The DOUBLE...
how does it work?

LUCILE AND JEAN-PIERRE GARNIER MALET

The DOUBLE...
how does it work?

Index

To understand the future, forget all that you have learned

In the morning, the sky is blue, the sun is brightly shining and happiness is singing in my ears. I am lost in my thoughts when all of a sudden; a ten-year-old young man comes up to me with a very decided step.

"It's over here!" he says.

He leads me to a house with an old, but cosy, facade. Sure of himself, he opens the door and takes me to the sitting room, tells me to sit down and runs out, leaving me somewhat disconcerted. A few minutes later, he comes back with my book[1].

"I was waiting for you impatiently" he says and sits down beside me, a little cross and lowering his head, adds "You know, your book is quite difficult."

"Have you read it?" I ask him disconcerted.

"Of course I've tried, otherwise I wouldn't talk to you about it," he answers, surprised by my question. "You say that we can change our future, but my mother keeps having a big problem with the future."

"A problem?"

"You say that she can resolve it without you needing to know it. I would like you to explain to me how I can change my mother's future."

---

1. Change your Future through the Time Openings.

This very serious young man both amuses and surprises me.

"Why do you say, from the first page, that if I want to understand everything, I have to start by forgetting everything I know? How silly! How am I supposed to forget everything? Shouldn't I at least first remember why I wanted to read you?"

"It's a question of forgetting what you think you know."

"So you should only say that if I understand your stories about time and forget mine, I change my future and have a quiet life."

He doesn't seem to want to confirm the surprise that can almost certainty be read on my face. His commentaries seem to me so surprising for his age that I am dumbfounded.

"My mother hasn't been able to find her balance despite having followed your instructions to the letter and having changed her life-style. Her problem is still there! My father says that she is completely off her rocker."

On the sly, he finally looks me in the eye, making me feel uncomfortable.

"This has made me think that if I, in order to see well, light a small lamp, then, if I see the illuminated one, meaning you, I will be able to understand."

It is impossible to keep being serious. I let go a loud chuckle.

"If you knew my mother's big problem, you wouldn't laugh. That's for sure!"

I try to recover my seriousness.

"Perhaps it is less serious than you think..."

"It's enormous. I'm her problem! I must resolve it and that's why I need you to explain how time works. I would also like to control the past and the future instead of standing stupidly by in serious situations. Tell me clearly how I can be the owner of my own destiny!"

I look at him stunned; in silence... My expression seems to surprise him, as it is now he who starts laughing.

1

There is no need to be a scholar

The child looks at me and sighs.

"You know you exaggerate when you say that no special scientific knowledge is necessary. Because of you, my mother has an inferiority complex. She isn't a scientist. It is very difficult for her to understand your stories about time. So I would like you to explain to me how to control the past and the future, if not I will leave the problem in your hands."

"I thought you said that you were the problem."

"Exactly! I would like to tell her: I am no longer a big problem because I know how to manage life. You say and write that: Doubling is a physical law that allows us to create the best future before living it. I want to create the best future, overall for my mother, but what happens is too hard. How do you expect her to manage?"

I am astonished to realise that he has tears streaming from his sad eyes. I feel bad for not having seen the bewilderment of this child whose seriousness no longer covers up his vulnerability.

"Since you insinuate that it is simple, okay, I'll listen to you."

He quickly wipes the tears from his eyes, sniffs and looks at me forlornly, while adding between sobs "You know? At first I thought that my mother was a waste of space, but now I think the waste of space is you... unless you tell me why I haven't understood anything when you say that everyone can understand you."

He sniffs again and smiles at me... a smile which in no way announces happy days.

"Your famous doubling, what is it? I have to understand it well so that everything at home can go back to being how it was before. Will you tell me?"

I am too moved and don't know what to say. As he sees me in doubt, he keeps on talking in order to win the match.

"You can do it quickly if you explain it to me, without those big academic words, just with simple words so that my mother and I can understand."

How could I refuse such a call for help?

2

Doubling Space and Time: How? Why?

I keep going, without knowing too well what I am going to be able to tell this child to satiate him.

"Doubling a space is..."

The boy interrupts me, "I've understood that part, you don't need to explain that to me. I have two goldfish that used to fight all the time. My father put them in separate fishbowls. Now I can compare their reactions. My father says that he has doubled the space of the fish. That's easy to understand; however, even he doesn't understand your doubling of time."

"Imagine that time does not go by at the same rate of speed in each fish bowl!"

He starts to laugh, "Do you think that fish watch the clock?"

"It is only a supposition."

"You should talk about frogs. My mother says that they are sensitive to weather."

The child talks with such seriousness! I discover nothing in his face that is not prey to his rapt attention. I clear it up for him with an amused air.

"It's not about the weather, but about the time that passes."

"I know, but the goldfish don't care about the time that passes or the weather outside. Rain or sunshine doesn't interest them, as they are always wet. Nevertheless, a frog comes out of the water when it's fed up. It knows that there is a time for each thing."

I make use of this unexpected commentary.

"A time for each thing, that is the simplest explanation! If you don't have time to study a problem and you need a solution to go on living, what do you do?"

"I would die," answers the child, satisfied with his response.

"Then you would die ignorant. On the other hand, if you had another space where time was not the same, a place in which a second of your time lasted several months, you would have time to find the best solution to your problem."

"Does that place really exist?"

"If it didn't exist, you wouldn't be able to live."

The child stars at me in surprise.

"Are you sure of what you are saying?"

"Each gesture you make causes a lot of problems to your body." I explain. "You adopt an immediate solution, without thinking, instinctively. You breathe, walk, eat and drink without need of knowing either how or why. Doesn't that seem strange to you?"

The young man's face radiates happiness.

"Cool. I'm going to study my mother's problem there where I have time and bring the solution back to where I don't have time. That is so great!" But his happiness doesn't last long. He immediately complains. "No, it's not great because it's impossible. I know perfectly well that I am always here and never in another place."

"Unless you have a double!"

"A double? Another kid like me? Then his mom must be very sad, like mine is."

"He doesn't need a mother where he is."

All a sudden I see him uneasy and annoyed.

"And my mother has a double?"

"Yes, like everybody else, your mother has a double, but she's not the mother of your double."

"Is this your real discovery?" he asks disappointedly.

"It's an important discovery given that in the universe, where everything is duplicated, it's the only form of life. You need to study your future possibilities there where there is time, so as to be able to make the best use of every second here where you don't have time to reflect."

I see him doubtful."

"If my double had found the solution, my mother would no longer have the big problem that I am."

"If you knew how to listen to him, you would have the solution. But you don't know how and neither does your mother, because you think it's complicated. Nevertheless, it is easy. It is so easy that nobody wants to believe it."

"If it's so easy, why don't you just tell me, instead of going on and on about a lot of things that do my head in?"

"I have to explain you things that are very complicated in the first place in order to prove to you afterwards that everything's very simple. Adults are made that way."

"I am not an adult."

"That's true, but you're not a baby either. A baby continuously uses her double as she needs him to live and because she still doesn't understand the chatter of adults."

A bright smile suddenly lights up the child's face.

"You know, my mother says that I'm still a baby. So you can tell me what a baby does with her double because I don't understand the jabber of adults either, but I need it to live!"

3

Dreams are Vital

This young person, a draft of a man, touches me.

"Your double can take care of you during your dreams. Only your way of going to sleep allows him to come to you in order to advise you and arrange your future possibilities."

"Is that all?"

"That is all. A baby knows it and lives without concerns about tomorrow."

"I wouldn't be surprised if nobody believed you, but you know, I like it. At least it's easy and simple."

"That's because you're still young. With older people, you have to hide simplicity by hardening commentaries with demonstrations made out of re-inforced concrete, because nobody wants to admit that the essential can be resumed in very few words."

"I would like to find in your explanations those very few words."

"They're there! The very first control of a dream, which by definition is uncontrollable, consists in knowing how to fall asleep attracting your double. If, like babies, you don't need an explanation about the exist-ence of this other you, you'll save yourself a lot of time. It's the thought process that slows us down. Have you ever seen an animal that stops to think before drinking?" This comment makes him smile, so I keep going "drinking time is just as important, it doesn't need any reflection."

He looks at me with an inquiring air.

"Drink time? Are you serious?"

"It's about drinking, while you sleep, information from the past and the future. That's why dreams are there. Have you ever noticed that they make us live in a time different from our own?

He interrupts me, "So, what my dad says is true."

"And what does he say?"

"He says that your stories of different times are gratuitous suppositions because they have no validity."

"When he knocks on your door to wake you up in the morning, you grumble, don't you, because he has pulled you out of a marvellous, and often, very long dream?"

He looks at me, surprised.

"How do you know that my father does that?"

"Tell your father that investigators, that means scientists, who at all cost want to avoid gratuitous suppositions, have realised with amazement that an extremely long dream with never-ending stories, can be caused by the noise that wakes up the person who is dreaming, that means almost instantaneously. The exact length of a dream can be timed by putting electrodes on our heads. This demonstrates that two different time flows truly exist, which are, nevertheless, simultaneous. So, tell me why this long life, in another place, wouldn't let us live well by finding our balance as soon as possible?"

"So, what do we need to do?"

"Know how to fall asleep, in order to be able to control our dreams. It is not complicated. If you don't do it, your dreams take you towards solutions that have nothing to do with your problems, and you spin around in circles."

"What do you mean by falling asleep well?"

His thirst for knowledge and his impatience surprise me.

"It is our double who takes care of us in our dreams. We must therefore first tell him all the problems that concern us!"

"But he should already be aware of them, since you say that he is me!

"He doesn't see us or hear us. He knows nothing about us. It is our body which records everything that we tell him. It's our body which passes on all the information to our double when he comes to us while we sleep."

"And then?"

"And then we go to sleep asking him his solutions."

"Is that all?"

I once again hear disappointment in his voice.

"See. You're already starting to grow up. You want explanations. A baby doesn't try to understand. She completely trusts her parents and easily falls asleep. She doesn't know about insomnia or thoughts that would lead her away from her double. She knows that when she wakes up she will have the information necessary to live well. If you have this certainty and this confidence, you will have the best solution possible to all your problems."

"That is too easy!"

Despite his tone of voice, I feel that he is invigorated and happy.

4

Moving causes us to grow old more slowly

He asks me insistently.

"If, during our dreams, we can take the time necessary in another time, what's it good for?"

"It's good for studying our future possibilities. We can then update the best of them afterwards."

"What does update mean exactly?"

"That, at each instant, we live in our time the future that seems correct. We bring it up to date instinctively."

"With me as her kid, my mom must have chosen the worst of all the updates." He adds with an annoyed aspect. "Do you really believe in what you say when you insinuate that by moving we grow old more slowly than the people who just sit around in their armchairs?"

"I don't exactly say that, but yes, that's true."

"My dad says that they are culubrations," he gets stuck on the word and after seeing my surprise, adds, "I like your culubrations." And paying no attention to my smile, he continues "To simplify it all and make it interesting, you mention Einstein and the relativity of time. I don't know what that is and my mother doesn't either. According to my dad, it is not something for my age and so he doesn't have to demonstrate that he doesn't know what to answer me."

"You think that you aren't able to understand Einstein and above all to apply a theory established by a great genius. Nevertheless, you are much wiser than you might imagine, as you already make use of this physical property in each instant in order to survive. The relativity of time is so integrated in you that you don't give it the least importance. You were born with it. You know it so well, it appears to you so logical, that you simply ignore it."

"I ignore it so well that I don't even see how I could use it!"

"By making use of the future! Like a stone that falls into a pond, Einstein's ideas about time splashed the entire world. At that time nobody saw any practical application in them. Scientists asked themselves: How could we not grow old at the same rate in all parts of the universe? They didn't at all consider clairvoyance, intuitions and foresight, so little rational to their way of thinking. Nevertheless, travelling in different times makes us dream. Scientists asked themselves silly questions, questions that were taken up by novelists and scriptwriters, for example: how can we turn into the father of our mother or in the child of our child?"

"Why did they do that?"

"If you imagine that you can go back to the past after living in the future, you can meet your mother before she gets married. If you loved her before the space voyage, it would not be difficult for you to fall in love with her, would it? So you get married and have a child. During the pregnancy, you go back to the future and find out that her child is you. You are your own father. Your mother, who believes you are dead, thinks that you are talking foolishness and that you are only your father's re-incarnation."

"That's mad!"

"Of course, but not mad enough not to be the truth! Science fiction and its suppositions were on the right track since nobody imagined that two identical watches could move at different speeds going further apart or coming closer together.[1]

The child sat staggered.

"Are you sure of what you're talking about?"

"It's been demonstrated.[2] A cosmonaut in his rocket grows older more slowly than we do." He doesn't believe it. An explanation comes to mind, though it seems difficult for a child of his age. "It's the acceleration that creates this phenomenon. If you travel in an ultra-fast rocket for a year, you can return to Earth two or three centuries later. Everything depends on the speed. Upon your return, your concerns and your language would give the impression of a far away past."

"That's cool!" exclaimed the marvelled boy. Suddenly he takes on a deeply sad aspect. "Yes, but if I leave now in a rocket, for, let's say, a year, my return would be awful."

"Why?"

"Octavia would be a little old woman or she'd already be dead."

"Who is Octavia?"

"She's my girlfriend," he states proudly. "She's really pretty, you know. But tell me, in the rocket, is it true that the hands on my watch would move more slowly than hers?"

"Of course!"

"That's amazing. Do you realise how many batteries I would save?"

"Speaking of watches..." I take a look at my watch, "Does your mother know I am here?" Her absence greatly surprises me. I had been expecting her arrival, often looking at the half-opened door.

---

1. See: Change your Future through the Time Openings.
2. In 1971, making use of atomic clocks, J. Hafele and R. Keating demonstrated that a passenger on an aeroplane does not grow old as quickly as he would on Earth.

"Yes, she's coming. You arrived really early and she hasn't had time to get all dressed up."

"She's the one who is late; you should go and tell her I am here."

"It doesn't matter! You've come to see my mother because of her problem and I've received you beforehand, since her problem is me. As my father says, it's a mannerly exchange, isn't it?

I smile at this child, who, without raising his head, pores over the pages of my book like an applied scholar.

What I didn't know was that behind the door, his mother was listening to us. She would have leapt upon me like a tigress if I had said anything out of place.

5

Observe and choose the future
before having to live it

This curious little man, lost in his thoughts, appears to be happy.

"I would like to be that cosmonaut that returns a year later to observe and choose the future before living it, provided that Octavia were in the rocket with me, of course."

My smile fades, but I am, nevertheless, perplexed as to this family's big problem and this child.

"Yes," says the child, "I would like to take a voyage in time where I go back to the era of stagecoaches and come back to today, discovering all the progress at once: cars, aeroplanes, telephones, computers...it'd be great!"

"Yes," I answer, "you go to a time in which they kill each other with swords and come back to discover a civilisation in which they kill cleaner and quicker with handguns and rifles, machine guns, cannons, atomic bombs and all the marvels of our civilisation where money has substituted the gods of our ancestors."

The boy stares at me like a duck looking at the knife.

"Are you serious?"

"Of course."

"You've forgotten the television, cinema, sweets and chewing gum that your cosmonaut takes with him in the spaceship. You know it's not easy to understand your story about time? It's complicated, but I like it. Cartoons are much simpler. You should try them."

He looks at me insistently, smiling and before I can say anything, he adds "I'd like to make that kind of trip. I could ask myself questions and find the answers where my spaceship lands."

"Now, imagine that you can come back just as fast as you left! Nobody will have noticed your escape and you will come back an excellent clairvoyant."

"If I came back too fast, I wouldn't notice anything at all."

"Of course you would, since a brief moment on Earth corresponds to several days there, where you go very quickly to live your dreams. There are always brief instants which we don't have time to perceive; they are called subliminal instants."

"You know, instead of using strange words that nobody understands, you should say what you just said to me. My father says that you should call a cat, a cat... even if you haven't got a cat. So, do cats have subliminal moments too, in order to leave and come back without anyone noticing them?

"Like all mammals, dogs, cats and men don't perceive these time openings because perception is totally discontinuous. We think we see all the time, but in reality we see successive images which give us the impression of continuous movement. In the cinema we see twenty-four images per second; the twenty-fifth is invisible. Nevertheless, it is registered in our sub-conscious. Advertising agents have made use of these subliminal images and have been able to prove, with satisfaction, that they modify the ideas of those that believe they don't see them."

"There are probably people who use these images to transform us into marionettes!"

"I'm sure."

The child smiles maliciously, "I would like to be able to do the same as them. Once I saw a film where a man moved so fast that nobody else had time to see him moving. He took off people's ties and belts, undid ladies' bras, it was funny, really funny..."

6

Between the light of the past and the darkness of the future, doubling is imperceptible

I want to look at my watch again, but the child covers its face with his hand while saying to me, "When I sleep, I know perfectly well that I don't move from my bed. I think that my father is right, your stories don't make any sense at all."

"At night we are all ultra-fast travellers," I tell him, "Our dreams drag us towards other spaces, at monumental speeds. Do you know why?"

"No."

"Now you see, you have another very light body that every night leaves your body that is sleeping. It travels much faster than light. That's the necessary condition in order to have two different aging processes! You live a long time there where you go, whereas here you hardly have time to observe your comings and goings. Your trip is imperceptible. There where you go, you live another experience in a time different from your own."

"But if I leave my body, it dies, doesn't it?"

"It doesn't even have time to realise you're gone. Besides, you don't think that your trip even exists, since, generally, you don't remember anything."

"But what is travelling so fast and so far good for, if you don't remember it?"

"In night clubs, there is usually a disk full of holes which spins in front of a projector; it's called a stroboscope. Turning it on, you see the dancers each time a hole moves so that the light shines through it. If the disk spins slowly, the sensation is of a slowed-down time. When the disk is speeded up, you end up seeing continuous lighting. Nevertheless you know that sometimes nothing can be seen. If your ultra-fast trip to the other side is carried out in a time of darkness, nobody will realise that you have left. This strobotic light exists everywhere. Our streetlamps go off and on fifty times a second."

"I don't understand why they don't leave the light on, instead of always turning it off and on, like mad people. My father hasn't been able to tell me why they do that. But he said something funny. Do you know what he said?"

He looks at me with such a malicious air that I have to ask him, "What is it that he said that was so funny?"

"According to him, you are the only one who is turned on all the time."

"Aurelian!" shouts his mother as she opens the door to the sitting room.

I jump up to greet her.

"Good morning."

"Good morning, Jean-Pierre. My son was so anxious to talk to you that I have left you two alone. Please, don't pay me any mind."

"Mum, listen to this. You're going to understand why I see things that don't exist for Dad," he says excitedly. "Every night I take off at full speed to have tons and tons of far-away experiences. I come and go so fast that my body doesn't even realise I have left."

"I was talking to your son about dreams," I explain.

"I thought so," she says in a soft voice while looking at her son.

"Aurelian is very confused these days because of the nightmares he's been having."

"Do you know why my nightmares are dark?" asks the boy. "Because I don't have time to know that I'm going."

Seeing the surprise on his mother's face, I quickly explain.

"Well, in reality, it all depends on the place where you go. Time can speed up or slow down. Dreams are luminous and nightmares are very dark. Everything depends on the luminous vibrations that are intensified in speeded up time, to the point of becoming very shadowy. There, where you see your future, everything is dark."

The child stares at his mother sighing and pointing at me with his finger.

"He's always like that."

"That's enough, Aurelian! You mustn't talk like that."

"But what I say is true" the child adds offended. "Anyway, his book is hard to understand, with sentences that don't make sense and you don't dare tell him so because you're afraid he'll think you're stupid."

"Your son is right, the words are complicated, but the law is simple."

In an effort to smooth over his mother's irritation, I turn towards the boy.

"If a second in your bed, turns into days where your dreams take you, you can say that time is speeded up. Do you know why you notice this acceleration?"

"No."

"Because everything around you is very gloomy."

"Even during the daytime?"

"Sure, since you are used to living in a normal time, completely different from the accelerated time that exists where your future potential is created."

"What is a future potential?"

"A car can move at 200 kilometres per hour. That's a potential that we don't normally make use of. You can be bad and that is also a future potential which you don't use when you are good. Your present is found in a terrestrial light so bright that in the future everything appears shadowy to you. You catch glimpses of possible futures that frighten you in a total darkness that often appears hellish."

"What should I do not to see anything? I am fed up with nightmares."

"You have to go where time is slowed down, there where your double lives. For him, you are the one who lives in the darkness on a planet that appears luminous. It is all a question of speed. The Earth travels a space in our solar system while our sun crosses another space in the galaxy..."

"While the galaxy," continues Aurelian raising his voice "crosses the universe."

"Exactly! The place where you live wraps you in a light which illuminates you. When you leave your body, you go where the light is no longer the same. If time is speeded up, everything will appear shadowy to you. If it is slowed down, everything will appear bright."

A knock at the door interrupts us.

I stand up.

"I should go."

"Please don't" says his mother also getting to her feet. "I'm the one who needs to go for a moment. Tell my son to come get me when you have to go or need to speak to me, but please, tell him how to get rid of his nightmares!"

As soon as his mother leaves the room, the child gets into a combat position and cries, proud of himself, "To the powers of darkness!"

I smile to myself.

"Did you know that our ancestors were completely aware that the hellish future was hiding in the darkness? They feared the hells that were lost in the night of time."

Aurelian looks uneasy.

"Do you think that a Prince of Darkness truly exists, all black and full of magic powers?" he asks.

"Light and darkness! It's creation: *and God divided the light from the darkness.* You see how the phrase from the Bible is a perfect physical reality. In the first place, the Creator creates the future at night and afterwards updates the best of it during the day. *And God called the light Day, and the darkness he called Night.*"

"And God saw that *it was* good! Like croissants for breakfast!" concludes the child with a happy smile.

7

Why do we double?

The young man quickly becomes serious again.

"My mother says that we are guided by the great beyond. My father laughs about this. He says that beyond everything, there is, of course, nothing, otherwise it would be in the everything that involves everything. Do you believe in extraterrestrials?"

"I think that all the stars must be inhabited. Why would we be the exception in the universe?"

"My father says that people who talk about extraterrestrials should be locked up with the lunatics, who are always seeing them. I know I am not mad and I know that a madman is someone who doesn't see the ones who are talking to him in his head. There are a lot of things and these things give us a lot of ideas."

"Our heads are made to listen to our double. Only there are troublemakers who use this in order to give us false information."

He looks amazed, almost scared.

"Are there troublemakers in space, too?"

"I've told you that during your dreams you leave your body and Earth at full speed. Anybody can do the same. You become an extraterrestrial while an extraterrestrial comes into you."

I see him suddenly turn pale.

"You mean that I turn into an alien? That's crazy! I can't turn into one of them, all gray, no hair, with holes instead of ears..."

"Of course not! I say extraterrestrial to make you understand that you leave Earth to go to another place. That is how information is transmitted in the universe. When you don't like the information, it becomes a nightmare and you wake up to get away from it. Nevertheless, if you use these voyages to take the place of your double and your double takes your place, your dreams embellish your life. In him you find your memory while he gives the best information to your body, which recuperates its vitality. When you wake up, you have healthy instincts and intuitions. And the nightmares disappear."

"Why doesn't he come and take them away every night?"

"He can only come to you if you ask him to."

"A bloke who falls from the sky, I can just see that! I saw a movie on the telly where the military shut him up to study him."

"If you were that double, you wouldn't be mad. Your arrivals would be imperceptible, subliminal! You would be an invisible observer of the dark place where, according to your advice, your immediate future are created!"

"If I am an invisible double, how am I supposed to be able to give advice?"

"If your double cannot give advice, his future, wherever he may be becomes risky since he can only live in his world updating future potentials created by you on Earth. If he wants to push away dangers, it is absolutely necessary that he guide you. He's got no other option. And to do that it is necessary for you that you may listen to him."

"How do I do that?"

"By making him come to you and listening to the intuitions that come from that! He fills your head with great new desires which make you react in the way that he wants you to. He frees you from past projects which troublemakers had left in your memory during nightmares."

"Do you really think I am going to hear voices, like Joan of Arc?"

"Everybody hears them but few take notice. We live thanks to the thoughts that continuously come to us from other worlds and other times to guide us. Without them, we wouldn't have instincts or intuitions or foresight."

"I can just see my dad's face listening to the voices that come from heaven."

"Your double knows that he is only a small outside observer of the poor, small Earthling that you are. You can listen to whoever you want and even forget he exists. Nevertheless, he is the one who knows what you must do on Earth. He travels through the universe, observing here and there the best future possibilities for you. He would like to indicate them to you since you are the one who creates his future on Earth. Do you now understand why he comes whenever you ask him to? Of course his voyages take time, but he travels quickly and his absences are short. Since 1989 the doors between the different times are wide open, and you know something, I am also speaking scientifically. Adults need that."

Aurelian looks astonished.

"That's a crazy story! But how can our double give advice to a person who, like me, doesn't see him and doesn't know he is there in the invisible?"

"If you know you are doubled, you make use of every instant. It is enough to know how to talk to him."

"But nobody knows that!"

"That's why everybody goes from one place to another without understanding life. Your double can come to you in a flash to guide you continuously. Listening to him, you always know that you create pleasant potentials that he will update when it is time, at the end of your doubling."

"I don't understand that very well. You mean that my double lives in another place, on another planet?"

"Your double has stayed there where you left him at the beginning of the last doubling cycle. At the end of this cycle which lasts 25,000 years, you must go back and unite with him. This end is near."

"And where is this place?"

"Each person has a star in the sky."

The boy starts to laugh.

"I think my father's right!" He sighs, trying to regain his composure. "He says you have too much imagination and I shouldn't follow lotus eaters."

"Tell you father that Plato says the same thing."

"Who's Plato?"

"A Greek philosopher who lived more than four centuriees before Jesus Christ. He said: Each soul has a star and he that leads a spotless life during the time accorded to him, will return to his star.[1]"

"Didn't they say a lot of silly things in that epoch?"

"Yes, the same as in this epoch and these silly things are what allow you to live well today."

But my small partner in conversation was no longer listening to me.

"You know your doubling story cannot work! There are thousands of millions of people on Earth. Are there thousands of millions of doubles capable of directing us and of advising us in this manner? This would quickly turn into Hell."

"It already is Hell! We listen to everything, to everyone, everywhere. Nevertheless, each one of us has, with no exception, a double capable of advising us, who lives in a slowed-down time. The ques-

---

1. Timaeus and Critias by Plato, Penguin Books 1971.

tion we should ask ourselves is not who receives the best advice on Earth, but how to receive advice from our double. He is the only one who is adapted to our case, since he is us."

Aurelian looks me thoughtfully in the eye.

"How can you know if my double is the one who should advise me? I can also advise him."

"He is in his light. You live in an accelerated time, which means in his darkness, which to you appears luminous. You are the one who creates his future possibilities. You have forgotten it, but he hasn't. You are necessary for him. He knows it, you don't."

"How have I been able to manage to arrive to my mother's womb?"

"That's too long to go into here."

He probably guesses my intention of looking at the time and puts his hands over my watch.

"Can you tell me in two seconds where I am going after my death, since you say that I am going to re-unite with my double."

"What do you want me to say? He will be there, wherever you go when you die, if you are able to re-unite with him. Your life doesn't appear in his time, he has, like you, imperceptible instants which allow him to exchange information with you. He will update to his life the best future that you have been able to create for him. Now you see the importance of your dreams."

"And if I create a bad future for him?"

"He will update a bad present to his life and as his life is yours after your death, you will live badly and he will too."

"But nobody has ever explained this to me," he exclaims frantically.

"Nevertheless you have constructed with him the body that animates you on Earth. You have done it in order to resolve personal problems. Some people need a century; others die in their mother's womb. Everything depends on your questions. If we can find answers more quickly being blind or psychically impaired, you will be born blind or psychically impaired. There is no injustice in our differences since we are what we have decided to be before being born."

"And if I die too soon?"

"Don't worry about that! If you are in constant relation with your double, he will protect you and you will die when the moment and the hour comes. For him, the answers to the questions that we have asked before our incarnation on Earth are necessary after our death. We must survive together in another place along with the adequate solutions. If we drive our body and our spirit down a dead-end road, we get unbalanced. If we look for useful information, we re-discover our balance that allows us to carry on with the research undertaken with our doubles."

Unfortunately it is getting late and I must go. Upon seeing him so sad, I promise to return.

"The same time tomorrow?"

"And tonight, what do I do?" he asks uneasily. "I haven't understood everything."

"Be like the baby that doesn't try to understand everything before putting it into practice. Start by telling yourself that tomorrow everything will have changed according to the desires of your double and that if he judges it best for me to come, I will be here."

"You just got here and you already have to go. You must have a real problem with time, I'm telling you! What use is it to tell me that the future exists if you don't even know how to tell me what I am going to do when you have left? Who knows if maybe, because of you, I am already ill in the future?"

I answer him simply.

"Ask you double! Do what our ancestors did who tried to domesticate the future so as to make it acceptable before drinking it! The omens, the oracles, the predictions, the fortune tellers, the prophecies with their specialists were at our disposition.[2] Listen and swallow all that occurs to you!"

Happy to see that I have shown no intention of wanting to leave, he concludes.

"I probably swallow such bad futures each night that I don't digest them. Some of them have a really bad flavour, you know?"

"You swallow, but you also create. We emit and receive information constantly and we are unaware of it. If we don't know how to classify it, we advance towards the future without driving codes, going through red lights all the time, counting on our good luck to avoid accidents. The future always opens a range of possibilities. It depends upon you to choose the best future and the least dangerous one, by following the advice of your double."

---

2. The caduceus was a symbol of Hermes' clairvoyance. Hermes was the brother of Apollo and the son of Zeus. In reality, it traces the double helix of the doubling movement. See Annex II of the book Change your Future through the

8

Drink an acceptable future in order to avoid stress

"You yourself said it" exclaims Aurelian, "if you know the future beforehand, either it's boring or it is very scary."

His questions came in a rush with the evident intention of forcing me to stay with him.

"If you know how to arrange the future, it is more important than predicting it, thinking of something pre-established," I answer. "We are not predestined given that we can change the future in every instant."

"What does predestined mean?"

"It means that we are not obliged to live the future that is offered to us. We can change it in each moment, if we know what is best for us! You see then that it is good to have instructions from our double in order to be at ease. You can't be afraid the day afterwards if every night you receive good information! It is enough to listen to your thoughts and intuitions during the day. They will be a reflection of the counsel of the night before."

"Every morning I wake up with a knot right here," he touches his breast bone, "and I'd like it to go away without having to remember my dreams."

"It's not a question of remembering your dreams or not, it's about suppressing those future possibilities which are inadapted to your organism. Without controlling your intuitions and instincts, the dangerous return of a forgotten future is inevitable."

"What forgotten future?"

"Everything that you have been able to think during the day and that you no longer remember. For example, you think about killing the cashier at the supermarket who makes you nervous."

"Especially the one from the supermarket across the road. She is so stupid and she thinks she's so clever. She talks to me as if I were a baby and I feel like strangling her."

"Of course you know that you won't do that, but the murder already exists in the future. Anybody can make use of this potential and commit a murder that only your thought has created. You will be partially responsible. Do you see the danger of a forgotten potential? You create a thousand volts and someone comes along and gets electrocuted by connecting to your potential because they can only stand two hundred twenty."

"My potential must be close to zero. I can't even eat. My mother doesn't make me have breakfast anymore, because I always vomit. Do you think that my double can take away my fear?"

"Only if you allow him to! It is difficult to know if your way of falling asleep is good. In order to find out, there is an infallible criterion: the next day you are no longer tense and you feel well. Our double always puts us on track, which doesn't create fear about tomorrow. Even though you have no memory, your body has received healthy information, it feels well and it tells you in its way, despite the fact that your head believes that things cannot change during the night."

"Have you ever seen anyone who was not at all afraid when they got up in the morning?"

"Of course I have! I have many examples."

The very depressed business owner comes to mind.

"It's too much!" said the person overwhelmed by problems, "my company is on the verge of bankruptcy, my wife has left me and thanks to my illness, I wonder if I don't already have one foot in the grave."

Not long after finishing our workshop he wrote to us.

"Finally a life without stress!"

Later on his business was back on track and his general health improved.

"But unfortunately his wife came back" adds Aurelian knocking himself out with laughter.

"They got divorced, but without a conflict."

"An ailing person is someone who is afraid of death, but I don't have a company or an illness. My mother says that I am too stressed out, but what is stress?"

"Stress is always the consequence of a problem without an apparent solution."

"I have a solution, but it is even scarier."

"Ask your double! If there isn't a solution, he will erase your problem."

"How? All at once?"

"It's possible. It all depends on you."

"And how can I find out?"

"By listening to him."

"I wouldn't mind being able to hear him!"

"You must pay close attention, his answer often arrives indirectly."

"In your book you give a lot of examples and you repeat many times this too much, too much, but I haven't got anything."

"You always have indications of too much, too much, as you say. It depends on you to see them. A book that falls open, a phrase on the telly, everything that you can perceive can be useful information. You must reconsider before rejecting as useless something you read, see, hear or I don't know what. You can trust in your double for everything and in every instant, if you know how to use him in your dreams. *I'll sleep on it* is a valid phrase that used to always be put into practice. Knowing how to interpret signs is a necessity for whoever wants to anticipate the best future."

"My dad says that in tennis, I know how to anticipate very well."

"So do the same in life! Knowing that the solution is found at the end of the road frees you from all anguish and allows you to look towards the future without fear."

"My mother has tried everything and hasn't been very success-ful. I still have my big problem. I can assure you that she has done everything. My father jokes that she has spent the entire household budget. Anyway the great thing about our double is that we don't need money to get in touch with him."

All of a sudden he seems so lost in his thoughts that I steal a glimpse at my watch.

The child notices this.

"And besides that he is not always looking at his watch. It runs too slow in his time."

I smile at him. He smiles back.

"My mother says that there are techniques that work on people who do not know your stories about time!"

"There are, but first you need to know why they work so you can eliminate everything that is useless and creates superstitions."

"Are superstitions useless?"

"They are. If you think that it is bad to sit thirteen at a table, walk underneathe a ladder or see a black cat, you create a bad future which will be updated by someone who thinks like you do. Something bad happens to you and a friend says: *Bad things never come alone.*

This automatically updates a second problem, which makes the first one worse. This friend is as dangerous as the one who mockingly says to you: *Never two without three!* And now you are hospitalised after having told everyone that they had warned you. This is how you augment the danger of superstitious."

"But everybody says that! I can't plug up my ears all the time."

"It is not by avoiding those who talk foolishly that you will escape the consequences of silly ideas and superstitions. You must ask your double to make a selection and optimise his techniques given that by ignoring them they can become dangerous while they apparently look effective. If you know nothing of the past and the future, what purpose do the gym, ablutions, hymns and dances have if not to entertain you? How do you know that if it is good to walk on coals, take drugs, immobilise yourself, go into a trance, ask God or the devil, pray to all the saints in heaven or light candles in churches? When you don't know anything, intuition is always less dangerous than superstition."

"You always say that it is within everyone's reach and I say that you exaggerate a little too much."

"It is easy to tell yourself that the day brings problems that we can resolve at night. Nevertheless, we prefer to think that we have no responsibility for our imbalances, that a condescending God watches over us or that bad luck pulls a face at us, when in reality we are always gathering the fruit of our way of falling asleep."

I look at my watch again. Aurelian complains.

"I will never understand it all, if, as soon as you get here, you have to go. If you spend a little time with me, your double won't reproach you for it since he, in his time, won't even notice it. So do me a favour, stay a little longer!"

"You are an incredible child!"

"Does that mean that you are staying?"

"I've got a lot of work..."

"If you take into account what I am saying, you can transform your book and so your readers will change their futures much more easily. You will not have wasted time since you will sell more books. As you will have more readers, you will have more potentials and will change the entire planet. There will be no more catastrophes and everyone will say: *Thank goodness he met little Aurelian, otherwise the Earth would already be destroyed.* And who will take charge of humanitarian aid when everybody needs help? Nobody. There will be nobody to take care of anybody. I can see all of the future evils that will be taking shape because of someone who wants to go as soon as they take a seat."

"You are now starting to understand my stories, little man."

I have received a good lesson, so suddenly I am in less of a hurry. With a half-smile Aurelian continues.

"You say that with our double, the next day is always better than the day we are living. It is always like that?"

"Yes, it is."

The child sighs.

"If I create a future like it should be, I won't have to be afraid anymore, but I won't feel like doing anything since everything will be all right. My father says that it's not worth having thousands of millions of pounds, because a multi-millionaire no longer wants anything, he has everything he wants as he buys everything that he desires.

"Choosing our future is not that easy!"

9

The Simplicity of Falling Asleep

This curious little man makes an interesting observation.

"If I have understood correctly, we are better off choosing a good mattress in order to get a good night's sleep!"

"Did you know that Pythagoras said that in The Golden Verses: Never suffer sleep to close thy eyelids, after thy going to bed, till thou hast examined by thy reason all thy actions of the day.[1] And that was four centuries before Jesus Christ."

"Who are you talking about?"

"Pythagoras. Haven't you ever heard of the Pythagorean theorem?"

Aurelian sighs.

"No, and it isn't a theorem that is going to make me understand better. My father says that you drag us through a labyrinth of complexity. What is a labyrinth of complexity?"

I can't help laughing out loud.

"Instead of laughing, you should help me."

"Complexity is the opposite of simplicity and to control our dreams, there is nothing simpler. First, before going to sleep, talk with your

---

1. The Golden Verses of Pythagoras by Fabre d'Olivet, trad. L.R. Nayan, Hermetica Press, 2007.

double and comment on all the things that bother you, without with-holding anything."

"Even very complicated problems?"

"Everything, even what you are afraid of."

"If I am afraid before going to bed, I can't go to sleep."

"Why be afraid if you are going to be given the solution? Besides that, you don't have to think about that right before going to sleep. You can do it a little beforehand. In the past our ancestors knelt in order to reflect upon their problems and so avoided falling asleep. Christians have made use of this position to pray more easily without exactly knowing why."

"My mother's grandmother had a prie-dieu in her bedroom. I could use that!"

"But why? It is useless to make a position comfortable, which in order to avoid falling asleep, must be uncomfortable. Besides that, you don't need very much time to tell your double your problems, you already know them by heart."

"And then?"

"And then you go to bed, if haven't done so already and always before going to sleep, ask your double to find the best solution to your big problem."

"Is that all?"

"That is all. It is even simpler still because you don't ask him for your solution but his, which may not have anything to do with yours. It will be a big surprise."

"Are you sure that my big problem is going to disappear by the simple fact of asking him for a big surprise?" asked the child, stupe-fied by such simplicity.

"If you are sure that your double is going to give you the solution, he will go look for it in your future. It is enough for you to trust in him and fall asleep without thinking of anything else. You close your eyes confidently, sure of the outcome."

"He has never answered me; I don't see why he would do it now just because I trust him and am sure of the outcome." Aurelian says disappointedly.

"If you don't go to sleep immediately, you are thinking about something else. In this way you prove to your double that you don't expect anything from him or that you are afraid of the future or worse still, that you don't want to know anything about his solution. When you ask your parents a question, you don't walk away before having their answer, do you?"

Aurelian reflects a moment before happily realising "But that is too easy!"

"Of course, since you have given up being complicated. If you confess your powerlessness, which means that you think that your double possesses a strength greater than yours. He is only waiting to prove this to you. Why do you want it not to work? He travels all around in search of the best solution and as soon as you ask for help, he immediately comes to guide you toward the best futures."

"And if he didn't have any good ones?"

"He would fix them before you could update them."

"Do I go to sleep when he comes or do I go to sleep so that he comes?"

"As you think of nothing else, you await his help and his response impatiently. Then a second later you fall asleep like a baby. You know that you are going to have a big surprise and that the next day will be better than the day before. Without knowing why, you wake up feeling well. Your big problem will probably have found a solution. In order to notice this, it is enough to live according to your instincts and your intuitions."

10

Be successful without trying to understand

The next day, as soon as I ring the bell, Aurelian opens the door and throws himself upon my neck. He exclaims, almost without air.

"Even my dad slept well! And now that I think of it, I haven't introduced you: my dad, Charles and my mother Francoise. I would have preferred Francois and Charlotte."

I smile, Francoise addresses me.

"I can't thank you enough. My husband and I have had a good night's sleep, we haven't woken up with the persistent anguish that we usually do."

"It's your double that you should thank. I had nothing to do with it."

Her son looks at me, intrigued.

"You said our sleep is paradoxical because we cannot move at all. Do you also think that I am paradoxical?"

"What do you mean by that?"

He quickly takes me towards the sitting room. His rush seems disgruntled or fearful. Once alone, he confides in me.

"When I have my big problem, I can't move; it's like I were paralysed."

Seeing my uneasiness, he smiles in order to reassure me, but I don't know what to think of what he tells me.

"They say it is psychosomatic."

Without awaiting my comments, he adds,

"Do you think that one night alone is enough to get information which can put back into order my disorder?"

"Your double is at your service all the time. He is only awaiting your invitation to transmit to you the best survival instincts. The only problem is that without controlling the way you go to sleep, your dreams give you wrong information."

"How is that?"

"Our world creates the future of our doubles so that they may survive. According to this same law, another world is therefore necessary to create our future. Those that live in that future lie in wait for us every night to push away our double in order to modify our thoughts."

"Why is that?"

"Because only our double knows the purpose of our lives. If the others are able to modify our desires, they can live as they please and in this way create for us a useless or even dangerous future. Otherwise they would be obliged to live as we want to and, of course, they don't have any reason to want to obey us. Information from our double can provide us with a healthy idea, whereas useless or dangerous information coming from those which create our future can make us survive by mistreating us."

"Will I have received bad information last night?" Aurelian asks, suddenly uneasy.

"When you wake up without stress or pain, but with happiness, you can be sure that you have gone to sleep well. There are other criteria to identify your achievements. When you talk on the telephone, you know that the other person hears you because they answer you. When nobody answers the telephone, it keeps ringing or the answering machine comes on. You know that there is a technique, although you don't know what it is. When you get used to it, you use the apparatus as you please. With the time openings, it's the same. You can find out who picks up, who hears you, who answers. You have points of reference that allow you to not be disturbed, to go directly to the point or amuse yourself as you like."

"What points of reference?"

"In your dreams, either you land in the darkness of your nightmares or in the light of your double. In the light, it is very hard to move, you feel all right, but heavy, in a body that is very difficult to put into action. In the darkness of the future, you are light, you fly through troubling shadows: you live a true nightmare but only a brusque awakening makes you see that. Fear freezes your veins. You need a certain time to be able to come back to the present. You have the sensation of having been a witness to or author of a drama of which you only retain a slight memory."

"And how do you not get confused?"

"In order to choose between the two, you must control your last thought before going to sleep, as this energy of attraction determines where you go. It's the same with the telephone; you have to call the right number."

Aurelian is surprised.

"My thought can call the wrong number?"

"Yes, it either sends you towards the future or towards your double. If you ask your double to resolve your problems, you attract him and your dreams will be marvellous. Falling asleep with a thought that will unleash the future is just as easy, but it is no good for anything except modifying your thoughts which cause you to have nightmares. When you are going to watch a television show, you don't think about anything, you don't invent any sort of story, you just wait to be surprised. How can you resist falling asleep when the only thing you want is to trust your double! Overall when you know that he is going to bring to you the best future on a silver platter."

"If I have to think of a ton of things before falling asleep, I am going to have my eyes wide open..."

"Just the opposite! The expectation of a big surprise and the certainty of it coming will lull you to sleep. Your confidence is such that insomnia disappears without problems, often quickly."

"Before falling asleep, I think of the next day, in the last movie I've seen. I like to think about cartoons I have seen, I make up stories and then I am dreaming..."

"Yes, but you fall asleep badly, because that way of entering into dreams drags you towards the future and the darkness quickly gives you bad information. Then your body warns you, you don't feel well. On the other hand, your double's information is adapted to the life that you have chosen together with him before being born: it makes you feel well. If your waking is not pleasant, you must be careful because during the day you could update dangerous futures, much more dangerous than before."

"Why much more dangerous than before?"

"Because the future feels threatened by your effort. He is the one who has made it fruitless. Nevertheless, when you manage it, you create and update the best potentials and in this way, you not only eliminate serious individual disorders but also large-scale planetary catastrophes."

The child is startled. It is not easy for him to see the relationship between his life and life on Earth.

"Do you really think that if my mother had suppressed our big problem," Aurelian says sceptically, "there wouldn't have been a tidal wave in Indonesia?"

"You get rid of your problems by letting your double change your future. If everyone did the same, all the doubles would arrange all the potentials and no catastrophe would be updated on Earth. But that is not the case. Anyway, it is no good wanting to appease the planet before having arranged your own futures. Whoever is able to get back into balance by themselves, wherever they are, will get the entire planet back into balance."

"My father says that a mosquito that spits on a forest fire does his job, the same as an elephant, even though he doesn't have the same trunk."

"That comparison is as true as it is beautiful."

"My mother thinks that your stories have nothing to do with mosquitoes and you have to be an elephant to carry them out."

I don't agree.

"A mosquito that reacts is better than an elephant which runs. Success concerns those who wish to listen to my stories."

Aurelian smiles indulgently.

"Provided that they are able to understand them."

11

Illness is a warning signal

The child has hurt my pride.

"If you want to solve a problem, listen carefully to what I am going to tell you and run see if it works. A small child doesn't know how to read the instruction manual of a television, so she will push all the buttons on the remote control until she gets her telly to work. This child-like candour and trust are absolutely necessary."

He doesn't understand why I am irritated. "You can't control a dream. Everybody knows that."

"That's why you must control the way you fall asleep. Tell yourself that it not a technique or an instruction manual, but a vital principal that doesn't need to be learned. You use it constantly just to survive. You will see how easy it is."

He protests and with amazement in his eyes says to me, "Do you really think that a big problem can be a simple problem? In school, it sure isn't, even the teacher says so. When I can't solve an exercise, it's because it is super-difficult."

"Careful! Simple doesn't mean simplistic. A baby isn't simplistic as she lives thanks to the vital doubling principle. She knows what she must do because she maintains contact with her double. That's why she is always sleeping, or almost always. Afterwards, unfortunately, we teach her to live badly. *Don't even dream it!* is all we know how to say to get her to come down to Earth and tow the line. Nevertheless, that is the best way to leave her defenceless."

"Going to bed solves everything. It seems too easy!"

"It is the only way to leave your body and propel yourself into the body of your double who comes into yours. This way you can exchange thoughts with him. It is enough to tell him your problems by telling them to yourself. Your body becomes aware of them... It records everything that you tell it..."

As Aurelian looks surprised, I add, "I am going to tell you how... After this special recording, you fall asleep and when your double comes to you, it discovers, within your body, what you have been able to or have wanted to tell him."

"But I don't feel like telling him what I'm worried about every night." He makes an unhappy face. I sooth him.

"As you know that you are going to have the solution, this shouldn't bother you at all. Thanks to your double, you have the certainty that tomorrow will be better than today. This absolute trust can only lessen your anguish and that well-known stress that ties a knot in your stomach. You go to sleep expecting a solution, without any other thought. If the Prime Minister himself came to answer your questions, would you say to him "Wait! I'm going to see if I've gotten mixed up on my maths homework."

Aurelian smiles, quite satisfied. "It's not my homework that worries me at night. Last night I was concentrating on my eyelids, waiting for the big surprise and I woke up this morning. You know, it's true what you say!"

"And what is it I say?"

"To live happily, live lying down!"

"At least it's less dangerous than street demonstrations to resolve your problems."

"You know what my dad says?"

"No."

"He says that going to bed is very dangerous since ninety per cent of the people die there."

"And it is even more dangerous since dreams are responsible for your future. You will never again be able to say: I didn't know! You shouldn't have listened to me because now you know who is responsible for your misfortunes."

"How cheeky you are to say that to me. I don't want to have a big problem nor be a big problem to my mother."

"And what do you know? With the futures that we are creating all the time, we never know who is responsible for creating who or what. Nevertheless, whether you want to be or not, it is always you who actualises the future of your choice. You are not submitted to a bad capricious fairy or a vengeful god. You are free and will be even more so, if it is your double who chooses the best update for you. Leave him at liberty, so you will be absolutely free. *'Thy will be done, on Earth as there, wherever he is, in Heaven.'* That is the only secret."

12

Help others in order to help yourself

"So your story about time is the same story as the priests', whom my father doesn't like too much, because of the big problem. He always tells my mother that evil is the proof that God doesn't exist."

"He doesn't exist in our time, because we are in his darkness. But that is another story. Your double is not God, only a divine piece that is strictly yours, personal. Only I don't have time to explain to you how it works..."

I try to get up, but in vain, he holds on to me. "I still don't know how it works," he sighs, "You haven't finished...please go on! I promise you're not wasting time with me."

It is difficult to resist his request.

"The best thing is not only seeing that it works but assuring yourself that it works. If your problem is big, there is no need for magic. You must address the most urgent things first. That is the advantage of having a serious problem. The alarm bell doesn't stop ringing. You grab hold of the branches, our double's branches resist everything, you can be confident that they won't break, they belong to a tree as old as the world."

Lost in the book, he no longer listens to me. I wonder what the true problem of this child, who is evidently so worried, is. I don't want to ask him, as only his double needs to know in order to find the best future and help him update it. If I try to find out, Aurelian will think, rightly so, that I am using a technique, whatever it may be, for which I need to know the how and the why. As this is not the case, I prefer to not satisfy what would only be trivial curiosity. What does this child expect from me exactly? He raises his head.

"If you leave too soon, my big problem might not disappear and you will be responsible for me," he comments seriously, then adds uneasily..."Does each time I think of something create it in the future?"

"Yes, since you are providing information which is immediately analysed, re-inforced and completed. In the future, they have all the time they need."

"I don't understand anything. You say that I have a double there where he doesn't have time to reflect and that I create the future for him on Earth, over which I have all the time. Do I also have a double where there is still more time to reflect?"

"There are a lot of people there, but unfortunately no double. I have told you that you are the one who creates the future for your double in your world, which for him is darkness. You can do it according to his counsel, which, for you, seems to come from a luminous place. The ones that create your future are beings that live in your darkness, which you illuminate with your thoughts."

"Who are these beings?"

"I've already told you, they are non-terrestrial beings. In the past, they spoke of spirits of the dead, of demons, nowadays we speak of extraterrestrials. The words change, but the law remains. If there was nobody to create your future, you would not be able to update anything to your present and you would die."

The child finds this strange and keeps quiet. "Wow! It's really dangerous to think about anything. If I don't think about anything, they don't do anything?"

"Yes, but you will die, because nobody creates your future possibilities. The worse thing is to think things that are not true because you immediately create true consequences of what is false. Words are even more dangerous since they can modify the potential of the person who listens to them."

"So, you are a very dangerous person." He looks at me and starts laughing before going back to the attack. "I wanted to know if my body keeps my ideas in each one of its cells."

"Of course! That lets it modify your instincts, sometimes handicapping you."

"Does it also keep the ideas of others too?"

"It keeps everything that it perceives, although you aren't aware of it. That is how each one of us modifies our future and everyone else's potential. It is, therefore, necessary that your double erases dangerous futures while you sleep."

"If everyone thought nice things, there would only be nice futures, wouldn't there?"

"Exactly! And by updating the best, we could even push away serious planetary dangers. There would be no more destructive earthquakes, no more devastating tornadoes, no more deadly tidal waves; everyone would benefit from it, ourselves most of all. You see that by controlling the future, our objective is very selfish."

"Helping others through selfishness, that is new!" exclaims Aurelian. "But I don't see the relationship between my problem and the tidal wave that killed so many people in Indonesia."

"The potentials of a place can be very dangerous. Indonesia and Sri Lanka have experienced horrible, fratricidal wars. Malaysia perniciously attracts foreigners."

"My dad says that they sell children to the tourists there; that a market exists like that. How much does a kilo of child cost?"

This question surprises me so much that I look at him without answering. He goes on...

"My father doesn't know, and as he doesn't know, he says that I ask dumb questions."

"Selling a child will make the parents wretched, who didn't want their child to be wretched. If they sell their child, how can we expect good to come out of evil? Creating evil, you can only harvest evil."

"My mother wouldn't let my father sell me! And when my mother doesn't want something, my father doesn't insist."

"It is not enough to not do evil. Creating good potentials allows your environment to be able to update them. That is how we can avoid catastrophes."

"There are a whole lot of children who have died. Nevertheless, they are not responsible for the wars nor for the markets for the tourists, are they?"

"Each person has been able to create very dangerous potentials before having been born on Earth. We've been doubling in the same space for the last 25,000 years. If I could, I would explain to you how the time doubling cycle in our solar system works."

"Yes, but you don't have time," exclaims the child with a sad and mischievous air and noticing my look, he adds "Don't worry! You know that you're mad, but I like your madness because it calms me down."

How can I not feel touched!

"Calming yourself down is not enough, you have to act because without this modification of our potentials, survival in our world will be hard-going, if not impossible, in the near future. We live, without realising it, with the weight of a tonne of collective, excessively dangerous futures. All the climatic, magnetic, thermal, tectonic, planetary, solar, galactic gauges are red hot. Paradoxically, we are not concerned in the least."

"That's normal; nobody knows why they have to sleep on it anymore."

"Nor why we wake up with so many intuitions!"

"If I dream like you tell me to, do you think that I will have intuitions too?"

13

Intuitions

I carry on the dialogue with this child who sits comfortably in his armchair, my book on his knees. His trust, his true interest, his curiosity take me further and further into my explanations.

"As soon as you start to ask yourself a question, the answer is already known in the future where other questions are then asked, unleashing answers in its own future, that is, the future of your future."

Aurelian frowns, "what do you mean?"

"The law of time is the same everywhere. The future is a strongly accelerated reality, which also possesses imperceptible time openings where time is again accelerated."

"Do beings like us live in an accelerated future, having their own future where other beings like ourselves live?"

"Let's say beings adapted to the surroundings that we imagine and that they try to create according to our thoughts. The future is an obligation, which we cannot live without! It is the reason that incites these beings to attract us toward their future after our death. To live and survive, a reality like our own always needs a future potential that it updates according to its necessities and desires. That's how intuition works! Thanks to the tremendous acceleration of time in the future, I can obtain the answer to a question that I haven't yet had time to ask myself. It is so fast that I have the sensation of receiving information that falls from the sky."

"Do you mean to say that I am always the author of my intuitions?"

"Yes, but without being able to know it since, in my time, I haven't even finished formulating my question. Intuition is a feat only for those that aren't familiar with the reality of information exchanges among the different times. The animal world possesses this sixth sense. Instinctive foresight allows them to survive each second. They use their best potential because they don't think it over. Modern man has totally forgotten this possibility because we consider intelligence to be better than instinct. We no longer know how to listen to our body."

"So tell me, is the present always a result of a future that our body makes use of?"

"That future has already been created by the past! If your way of going to sleep is good, your double can transform it the best way possible before you may live it."

"So we are only machines for creating, arranging, controlling and updating the future?" Aurelian sadly concludes.

"Yes, but everything is possible while you look for the objective that you have established together with your double, before having been born."

"Do you think it is easy to have an objective? Till yesterday I didn't even know I had a double. I wanted to be a fire-fighter and today I still feel like being a fire-fighter. Do you really think that my double wants me to be a fire-fighter?"

"Don't worry; everything comes in its own time. If you listen well to his information, making sure that it is his, you will soon find out."

"How can I be sure? Because sometimes, I don't even feel like being a fire-fighter."

"Your double's advice will always fill you with an intense joy. In the past, the Greeks spoke of teoforia, the happiness which comes from God. These personal criteria that your body feels in each one of its cells will never lead you astray. It is an instinctive happiness and the intuitions that you receive at the same time are always the best. You can also memorise unpleasant situations from the future so as to avoid them. But be careful! This memorisation can bring about stress, if in it you see an inevitable reality, a predestination that disturbs you beforehand."

"My father says that we can't avoid the unavoidable. It's destiny."

"Apart from death, which is the fate of all human beings on this earth, there is no destiny, no karma, no predestination. There is no coincidence either, all is written in advance since your future is at your disposal in each second, but you are the one that chooses it before updating it."

"How do you do that?"

"The future has always been created by someone before you update it. You choose this updating because you think like they do."

"But that is silly!"

"A happy thought of a quarter of a thousandth of a second is enough to create happiness in the future. A similar thought can allow you to update this happy potential. Nevertheless, it is necessary that your body be able to hold it."

"I can't know beforehand," protests Aurelian uneasily. "For me to live a future without problems, it would be necessary that nobody creates hateful futures."

"Overall, it would be necessary for you to begin by not creating the least detestable future."

"So, I am responsible for the person who updates to their lives the futures that I create?"

"Only partially responsible! I've already explained this to you. The updating doesn't depend on you. Anybody can do it; it is enough for them to think the same as you."

The child takes on a grave aspect. He realises all of a sudden the consequences of each one of his secret thoughts. "But that is tremendous! I share a great responsibility!"

"Great or sensational! Everything depends on your thoughts, which can be terrible or fantastic."

14

One sole piece of advice:
Never think of doing to your
neighbour what you would not like
him to think of doing to you

"How do we do it so as to avoid the terrible and keep the fantastic?"

"We were given a piece of advice a long time ago..."

"Advice! Nobody can give advice when nobody knows your stories."

"Everyone knows this advice because my stories, as you say, were well-known a long time ago, but currently nobody sees their usefulness."

"So tell me, what is this fundamental piece of advice?"

"Never think of doing to your neighbour what you would not like him to think of doing to you."

Aurelian lets out a disappointed sigh. "Do not do unto others what you would nt want others to do unto you," he repeats. "That's known, super well-known. All the Christians repeat it time and again, but that doesn't change anything on the exterior."

"Because *do not do unto* is insufficient advice! The only valid and fundamental precaution is: *do not think of doing.* That is very different. Everyone knows what you do, but nobody knows what you think of doing. Some people will make you lovely gifts when, nevertheless, they only think of tripping you up. In other times these people were called *bleached tombs.* A nice expression: pretty on the outside, stinking putrefaction on the inside!"

"Anyway, your fundamental advice is not enough, because without knowing it, I can think of good things that create bad things in the future for others."

"That is why we need the double who, each night, must erase the dangerous potentials created during the day, before someone can update them." My small conversation partner stares at me uneasily, but momentarily satisfied with my answers. Then I add "Besides that, you once again find the thoughts of your double, which are your own and correspond to your body. Our cells feel at ease. Those that feel useless or dangerous kill themselves, so as to not disrupt the others."

"They kill themselves?" asks the child, both surprised and amused.

"If you forbid them from killing themselves, they can develop archaically and cause you to die."

"How do you expect me to keep them from killing themselves?"

"When your thought is no longer adapted to your body, your cells no longer know if they are useful or not. Their suicide or survival then becomes problematic. So now, this adaptation is only possible with your double...and providing that you allow him to go visit your future during your dreams! Then none of your cells will survive or die without having been useful for something."

15

The Mix of the Past and the Future

This child, very mature for his age, goes on. "Cells that commit suicide? That is amazing, but not too scientific."

"The scientific word is *apoptosis.*"

"There are some that can kill us, aren't there? My music teacher has got cancer. Is that because he is losing his mind? Maybe his cancerous cells have a bad memory, just like him!"

"And if these dangerous cells were looking for a potential inadapted to his way of life, created in the future by his upsetting thoughts? Information that has to do with their uselessness in our time and in our world should give them back the desire to disappear. And sleeping is just the natural source of this healthy information. As sleep makes us travel outside of time, we need to know the driving code, of the past and the future in order to always be sure of living well in the present."

Leaning over the book,[1] putting his index finger against his lips as if to silence me, Aurelian continues. "Listen to what is written in your book! *An ailing person in a grave condition... cancer dragging him*

---

1. Change your Future through the Time Openings.

to the tomb... intestinal occlusion... Once her stomach was opened, the surgeon could confirm the disappearance of the tumour. What do you want to prove with this story of healing? Are you advertising yourself?"

I find this question irritating. "I only want to show the fragility of an ailing person who, doubting the strength of his double and also perhaps the usefulness of his doctor, runs the risk of a relapse. Why do you want me to advertise myself? The best publicity is the one you do by changing your future. In this way, you create a good potential where before you created a bad one and everyone that makes use of it feels better and better."

"If I say what I say," exclaims Aurelian who feels my irritation, "it's because that is what my father says, but he doesn't dare say it to your face. I'd like to tell my father that your book can really change our future. That it's not publicity! That if I understand, I can push away my big problem, which doesn't have anything to do with illnesses. That's all."

I feel that he is about to break down crying and I feel bad. I continue. "In this book we have given examples in order to show that it is possible to get well. As I know that is difficult for us to admit that regaining our balance can re-establish a body worn-out by a long illness, I try to prove that there are no miracles. What is arranged with time in the future can instantaneously appear in the present. Nevertheless, we have to try to arrange the future before it starts being a bother."

"I've understood all that!" sighs Aurelian. "I've even understood that our double lives in a past that is as present as our present because every night he waits to see the future that I create for him and that it is as present as our present." Proud of his analysis, he carries on. "Nevertheless, if he thinks before I do, in order to influence me, he also lives afterwards, since he updates what I create for him. This changes his ideas, he asks me other questions and I create other solutions for him. Conclusion: we live at the same time." Happy with himself and at ease, he continues, adding "Do you know that you and your stuff are complicated? I'm not surprised that neither my mother nor my father understand anything. Nobody knows that story about time!"

"That is why the future that we create on this earth might not have anything to do with the one that, together with our double, we had decided upon before separating at the moment of our doubling."

The child is absorbed in what he is looking for and now reads aloud. "The future is as present as the past...All infants know this..." He looks at me with scoffing eyes. "Infants know more than we do? That's a heavy wager!"

"Of course! Nevertheless, their problems are different. They must adapt themselves to our time and space. For you, the adaptation is different and you can use your paradoxical sleep to try and get rid of an illness, maintain a romance, make a worry disappear or find money. But it is not enough. To impose order on disorder, you must change your way of living and thinking at the same time."

Without appearing to be listening, Aurelian continues the reading that I have interrupted and adds "You also say that the future exists before the present and that our double can arrange it. The future is one thing, but what do we do with the present? Our double should guide us all the time, overall when we are very afraid. But why does he abandon us as soon as we are frightened?"

"Because he only helps you if you ask him to and if your trust in him gives him the freedom to move. It is a law, which protects you, if not you would always be obliged to obey him. You would become his marionette and he would always know beforehand the future that you create for him. You would predestine him and he would get bored. Living and reliving the same thing time and again is not at all exciting."

"Then with the future, it is the same. Those that create it are not obliged to obey me. They do what they want in the darkness and perhaps think of me abandoning them."

"Exactly! But they can also give you misleading information, change your thoughts and draw you away from the concerns of your double. He is the only one, thanks to his questions and your appropriate answers, who can assure your survival after death. The others attract you in your dreams to change your thoughts and transform you into a marionette. They also know how to erase the bad memories that would make you run from them, substituting these for images as pleasant as they are treacherous. They know how to hide your nightmares under three good layers of marvellous dreams."

"They are brilliant! That is why you say that dreams are necessary but their memory is dangerous. Got it!"

"Information from your double never confuses you; it is always healthy, very concise, goes directly to the point and never talks bad about anybody."

"I understand that, but why is it useless to memorise our dreams?"

"Our dreams can drag us towards new nightmares. They haven't been conceived to cure imbalances, but to avoid them."

In a serious tone he stresses "My father says that life on Earth is a sexually-transmitted deadly illness."

I laughingly add "He is not the only one who says that! It's a way of realising that our problems often don't find a solution."

16

A Little Publicity

My explanations don't tire Aurelian, whom I already consider to be more of a young man than a child. He misses no detail and tries with all his might to soak up all that I can teach him.

"If I were you" he says "if I needed to advertise, I would do it only to show that your story can be applied to anything, by anybody..."

"Listen, this is important! My stories, as you say, allow you, together with your double, to look for a personal balance, to put back on track a wandering mind or a romance that is going down hill, as well as an unemployed failure or a disastrous bank account."

"Of course! We are completely responsible for our happiness or our unhappiness. We mustn't complain, we must only change our future! You give a ton of heart-rending examples in your book! I like the disoriented step-mother a lot, with those horrible children. My mother says you could draw tears from a crocodile."

"What example are you talking about?"

"The woman whose husband killed himself when he found out he had cancer and whose children didn't want to pay her back...you know...a week later the children delivered a check to her."

"Yes, now I remember! She couldn't believe it. It only took ten days to find a solution to eight months of costly proceedings and useless worry. She was also able to little by little quit taking tranquilisers.

Thanks to this extremely depressed woman, I discovered that substance dependency, be it tobacco, alcohol or drug related can also be annulled. Other participants in my workshops have subsequently confirmed this for me."

"This should be advertised!"

"This works perfectly, if the people with dependencies are few and isolated within a fairly large group who offer them a different potential."

"What do you mean?"

"If you bring together people with the same imbalance, you reinforce their problem by often giving them a potential too heavy to digest."

"Tell me about the forty-year old woman who was bored in Florence, alone, without a husband, without children or friends, who meets up again with her boyfriend from 20 years before." Seeing my lack of memory, he adds "You know it's the story of the Canadian who found his old agenda, which fell open to the page with the telephone number of his old girlfriend who had just been dumped. It's too much!"

Imagine this woman's surprise when she heard the voice of her long-lost love.

"It's not necessary to talk about the end of the story, we can guess it. You should say however that it is not so easy for everybody. For example my mother and I can't seem to get on our feet..."

"And you sink because you put limits upon yourself. You know that you can jump over an obstacle one metre high and you don't try to raise the bar any higher. In almost all cases, we are the only ones responsible for our failures. Have you read the story of the lady with multiple sclerosis?"

"What is multiple ske-lo-sis?"

"It is a serious illness."

"People are going to say: It's too good to be true," says the child, "and you will answer them: *No, it is by controlling your dreams that allows you to get out of an unpleasant or hateful situation. It is as easy as that!* Then quickly, without giving them time to recover, you will talk to them about that man who had an enormous debt…He was desperately playing the lottery and finally his banker pardoned his debt. Amazing, isn't it?"

"Yes, but you have to be careful, because it's dangerous to give examples. People can think that they can obtain outcomes equally as spectacular and the future will prove them right and…"

The child interrupts me. "Yes, but you have said that the important thing is to say what people can do, although later on they might not do anything. Let's go on! I like it when you talk about the woman who had lost everything: health, balance, work, flat, car, money, boyfriend, and gets through thanks to her double."

While we talk, I realise that he has used bookmarks to signal specific pages, demonstrating that he has read the book entirely and conscientiously. He finds what he is looking for and continues. "She was so depressed that she had decided to kill herself. After a good night's sleep with her double, she turns on the telly to watch her favourite programme, mistakes the channel and hears: *Suicide is never the solution.* Brilliant! It's just that anybody else could have told her the same!"

"Although it seems strange, it was the right answer. In the depths of her being, she knew that and nobody could have told her the same thing with the same force. Thanks to the new certainty and personal confidence, her life totally changed. You see that we have to observe the signs that we receive and not believe in coincidence. The book has many examples to show how changing our future is within everyone's reach."

I like the Chilean corporal who disappears for five minutes into the sky. When he comes back his has a five-day beard. What madness!"

"That demonstrates that we have another time within our time and that controversies are useless."

"What do controversies mean?"

"It means that it is not worth doubting."

"It's better to say it like that. You are so complicated!" he adds laughing.

17

The Physical Body
and the Energetic Body

The child gets serious again. "There is a thing that I haven't understood very well. You say that during my sleep I go to another place, at super-speed, like lightening. Nevertheless, I know that I don't leave my bed."

"You know that besides your physical body, you have an energetic body; some people call it an astral or etheric body. This body moves very rapidly and comes back to juxtapose itself with our physical body in an imperceptible time. Besides that, the water in our body keeps and transmits vital information gathered during these trips so as to allow us to go on living. Those who bring into question homeopathy should become aware of this universal reality: it is impossible to live without water and without a spirit, so said Jesus as well as Mohammad."[1]

"Do you know that when we are born we are made up of 65% water and when we grow old only 55% remains? The foetus, which needs so much information for her survival, is made up of 96% water."

Aurelian looks at me with his eyes wide open, befuddled. "Where do you see the water in our body? We are solid, not liquid."

---

1. See sacred texts.

"Our organism is a sponge full of water, stored in different forms. It is a laboratory where chemical reactions are carried out with water. Our energetic body informs the water of our physical body. It is a pity that science is not concerned with this fundamental part of our organism, as it is our undulatory side which allows us to emit and receive information. It is what gives life to our physical body. Being perfectly observable, it is no more than our corpuscular side. In the past, more realistically, the word *dust* described it better than current physics."

"When my grandfather gathered mushrooms, he always said to them *Dust thou art, and unto dust thou shalt return, but in the meantime you are going into grandpa's stew pot.*" It is good to hear him laugh. "Is our double also made out of dust?"

"Like us, he possesses a physical and an energetic body. His role is to find the best solution for adaptation in each place he wants to go. The physical body is obliged to live in our space, while the energetic body has the commitment of receiving the information that helps it to live. We can exchange our energetic body with that of our double, to understand our respective situations and try to live better *a deux,* each one in their world and time."

"What happens when my energetic body travels?"

"It leaves your physical body, nothing more. Some people call it *doubling.* The most realistic and the ones that are more used to this type of phenomena, which they call *normal* are the Tibetans.[2] They denominate it *the small death.*"

"Why small?"

"Without an energetic body, the physical body dies. But if everything goes well, our double's energetic body comes to us and our body revives."

---

2. See the Bardo Thodol or Tibetan Book of the Dead.

"And where has our energetic body gone?"

"Our energetic body keeps our double's physical body alive. This is how we re-encounter our questions, while our double becomes aware of our answers and quandaries."

"But how do you expect to use an energetic body that you don't see?"

"To watch television, you don't need to know that invisible waves, which vary according to their frequency, are transmitting the sound and the image. If you throw a stone into the water, you will see the displacement of a circular wave, which is the wave of the stone: the bigger the stone, the larger the wave. This is the way the stone says to the fisherman: *Look how big I am, see how your boat moves!* That is how a wave can displace and provide information by the wake it leaves. You don't see a ship in the distance, but on the calm waters where your boat sails, an immense wave is coming to wake you up. Waves cross each other, sometimes deforming initial information. Your boat can receive the small wave from the stone and the wave from the ship at the same time...It is difficult for you to believe in the stone's existence, but without it the wave would not be the same."

"Would this be how the wave of a tsunami indicates to you that there has been an earthquake under the sea?" asks Aurelian.

"It is a very fast wave. Nevertheless, when they are small they can add up their effects and bring about catastrophes. When you tie the end of a string to one point and you shake the other end, you create waves that vary according to your desire. A stone in the water also creates waves. It is important to understand the vibrations emitted by our body, as they are like the stone in our world and a wave in the other, where only the information that they carry appears."

"Does this mean that in my dreams, with my energetic body, wherever I go, I don't look the way I am?"

"Perception varies from one world to another. A bird on a branch sees the wave of a small fly on the still surface of a lake. It divines the imperceptible body due to the wave effect. It knows perfectly well that before it lies a good, consistent breakfast. In its world the little fly can capture the undulatory thoughts of the bird and the lurking danger and therefore tries to camouflage itself."

"So it's dangerous to change worlds...?"

"That's why we must know how to direct our energetic body during our dreams and go to the physical body of our double, who will then take the opportunity to go to see the future in our place. He will take care of sorting out the dangers. It is very important for you to know your problems well. Before going to sleep, you must then tell them to the water in your body as if it were a recording device. Tell it everything that seems useful. When you get lost in a big city, you ask for directions from someone near at hand; you don't stand looking them in the eye without saying anything."

"I am not stupid" the young man exclaims.

"Do you think you are more intelligent when you go to sleep without communicating with your double? When he comes to you, he must be able to understand the thoughts that your body has recorded. He can't know you if you hide a part of yourself from him. He can only help you if he knows everything about you; otherwise he can drag you towards serious dangers through ignorance. As he doesn't want to do this, he stops advising you and you live completely at random."

"Do you mean to say that my double abandons me if I don't speak to him?"

"In case of mortal danger your double will always be there. He needs you to be able to arrange your future his way. He is the one who best knows that coincidence does not exist. He knows that your present is the updating of a future potential, already lived more quickly in another place. That is the way your body's made. To survive he gathers information from the future that he can capture in his present."

"So I should obey the future! That means that Dad's right when he says that if I do something bad, I have to pay the consequences, that it's my destiny."

"Unless you repair the bad things in the future, before having the need of using them in the present! Your instinctive updating is always personal; it's your apparent coincidences that only depend on you and on your projects. Thinking of a future makes it come to life, thinking it's impossible suppresses it. If you think that God has a long beard and big ears, then later on you will always be able to prove to yourself that your belief is trustworthy because you will up-date a potential future, which your faith or the faith of those around you, will have created in the past."

"Does this mean that clairvoyance allows me to see what I want to see and not what in reality exists?" concludes the child who pins me down with questions, probably to delay my departure.

"You have understood well! Clairvoyance is very dangerous. The person who is able to see future possibilities often thinks that this future is unavoidable, obligatory. He feels happy to predict an incident that is carried out afterwards. What really happens is that he doesn't realise that he is the one who update this future. Without him that potential would probably have remained in the darkness. He should see dangerous futures only so as to be able to avoid them. A good clairvoyant is the one that predicts serious occurrences that never happen."

Aurelian shrugs "In that case nobody would go to see him, seeing a dangerous future that never happens is too easy."

"That's why a man whom has had an accident predicted for him finds himself happily in the hospital, clamouring to his friends: *Go see this clairvoyant, he's magnificent! He predicted that I would go through Hell after having a serious motorcycle accident. I didn't believe him and didn't even have a motorcycle as I always go by car. But it was a motorcycle which knocked over the scaffolding where I was working.* The man feels satisfied and he tells everyone about it."

"That's normal, he hadn't read your book," exclaims Aurelian with a mocking air.

His comments make me smile to myself. "But you should also know that you can always create one future in order to erase another. You modify your thoughts, your wants, your desires and you change your future. If, besides that, you allow your double to arrange your future each night, each morning a multitude of pleasant potentials will be at your disposal."

"Is what you write true or do you only write it because you think that it's true?"

I understand what he wants to say. In fact there are many people who ask how it can be that a scientific theory leads to such certainties!

"A person who has a head on their shoulders, who calls you on the telephone, doesn't ask themselves silly questions like: *Does the telephone work because I believe it does?* They simply make use of the apparatus. With your double, you should do the same. First you call, then you listen to who speaks to you and you try to recognise their voice so as to not be fooled. There are many troublemakers in the future that make use of this way of communicating to drive you up the wall."

"There are troublemakers everywhere!" points out Aurelian, who seeing me get up goes back to his silent reading as I have decided it is time to go. "You are not going without giving me an explanation of how I can get rid of the troublemakers by using the communication exchanges with my double. I am really interested in that! You say that we knew how to do it at birth because we lived with the carefreeness of a child who doesn't see anything paranormal in her surroundings. And you want to go, leaving me with the paranormal?"

"You are a paranormal phenomena! How can I resist without running the risk of a tsunami in the future?"

Such a large curiosity in such a small man couldn't help but greatly surprise me. His simple questions and his sensible comments impelled me to consider it a responsibility to satisfy them. It was becoming obligatory for me to instil in his small head short, precise answers to all his questions. This young man continued to surprise me, as much for his brightness as for his way of analyzing the smallest detail.

18

The Dangers of Intellectualism and Irrational Rationalism

Suddenly the child's countenance turns stony. "You put a damper on everything" he says turning around, "I was just about to find out the most important."

His father has just come into the room where we are. Very sure of himself and with a decided air, he firmly shakes my hand at the same time asking me to go on and not worry about him.

In this fraction of a second, I think I see in him the *superior intellectual type.* This is the favourite name that we give to the person that will never use an apparatus before having taken it apart, understood it and put it back together. In general, the homo-sapiens habilissimus soars over false problems in search of solutions that don't exist. They consent to listen to others only when they have a truly serious problem. The most intellectual and most superior can not avoid desecrating everything, giving the sensation of wanting the butter, the money from the butter and, at times, its process of fabrication. His mark of recognition is often ignorance which hides under intolerance towards those that might discover it.

This man, polite indeed, shows signs of certain hostility towards me. I prepare myself to pass an exam, but with an advantage over him: I can leave whenever I want to, unfortunately leaving his son in the lurch. As this child has struck my inner chords, a hurried exit would deeply pain me.

He has just sat down and he goes directly to the point. "In your book *Change Your Future,* you say on page seventy-eight: *we are the only ones responsible for our misfortunes and our happiness.*"

I try not to show the deep annoyance that invades me. "If you have read the previous pages, you will know that we create a dangerous potential: to understand conveniently the dangers of the future, let's say that we create 2,000 watts when we are made for 220. Why are we puzzled when we receive painful shocks making use of the only available potential for survival?"

"I am not against this idea that you have already expressed to Aurelian, after all our electric appliances work thanks to a potential created in the power stations. We have no need of knowing how these plants work to be able to connect our electric shaver or kettle! Why wouldn't it work the same for the future? What happens is that nothing proves to us the pre-existence of that future and much less the existence of beings capable of creating it for us!"

That's it! This father seems to me more worried about his intellectual problems than his son's problems. I keep calm.

"There is no need to know who creates it. It is enough to know how to regulate our survival potential. It is so extraordinary that it often appears paranormal, but in reality, only our ignorance is.

"If I wanted to see you today before you were with my son, it wasn't to bother you with stupid questions, but to find out what you think about healers. You state that everyone has come across, at one time or another, a person capable of taking away warts, curing small burns, moving objects, all the stories that you read in the tabloids."

"You have forgotten the people who find springs, that divine the future, that put joints back into place, that sooth pain or expulse demons, all of this without speaking about the healing that is considered miraculous. Aren't you surprised to see all these quick and astonishing healings?"

I felt that like many of us, he doubted the reality of such energy, ignoring that our body demands it every instant for its survival. So I didn't think it strange when putting the book on top of the desk, he asked me "What energy are you talking about?"

"The energy that each and every human possesses, although they don't know how to exactly define it. In other words, we can say that it is an energy that leaves us completely renewed."

"If you make use of it, do you think that Aurelian can make use of it too? Not everyone is a healer."

I object. "I am not a healer either! The objective of wanting to change the future is not for a healing, but the search for balance. It is more important to find the cause of an imbalance than that of the healing, overall when it takes on the appearance of a divine miracle. An illness is an alarm bell, curing it without looking for its origin is useless. If the cause doesn't disappear, another illness will come, perhaps a more serious one, that will make us regret the past healing."

I would like to talk to him about the dangers that stalk the healers, the confessors, the therapists, but I consider it useless. What I didn't know is that this "superior intellectual" had begun to be domesticated.

"Can you answer my first question now? What does a good healer do?"

"Heal without having learned how to do it. Judged beneficial by their patients, but dangerous by doctors, authorised healers, but often powerless, these sometimes spectacular healings are excessively dangerous for him."

"How is that?" asks Charles, very surprised.

"The person, who takes charge of a future of another person, can free that person of an imbalance that has been caused by the updating of that future. In that case he could say, like Jesus said to the paralytic: *Rise up and walk!* Advising you at the same time: *Your dangerous potentials no longer exist."*

"Do you think that Jesus took charge of the paraplegic's future?" he asks puzzled.

"I think that Jesus knew that possibility since the Greek language of his time spoke of it clearly and that this great *doctor of the law* of space and time could not help but know it. In this very old language creating a dangerous potential is said *amartanou,* which means to sin.[1] Of course, it's not about the sin that Christians consider nowadays. Taking charge of a sin heals an ailing person or resolves the problem, but it doesn't erase it. The healer then finds himself with a dangerous potential, a *sin* that he should suppress so that it is never again updated by anyone, if not he will be responsible for new misfortunes. By becoming his, this potential will be a temptation for him. He must then ask his double to *lead him not into temptation but deliver him from* that future *evil."*

"I had already figured that the Lord's Prayer was a favourite of yours."

"It is not a prayer that you recite mechanically. It is a natural and deeply reflected upon request from a son who knows, through universal law, or say, with certainty, that he has a *Father, in a realm which is not in this world, said Jesus, the author of this petition. So it is really not about* healing, but about the search for a healthy spiritual balance."

---

1. For the ancient Greeks, sin was $\alpha\mu\alpha$-ρ-$\tau\alpha\nu\omega$ (ama-r-tanou = sin): $\alpha\mu\alpha$ = ama, which is the doubled α, with the best present state, μ, between the past α and the future Ω. The link r = ρ of the doubling of α can immobilise us or hold us back (tano).

19

Anticipation or the Power
of Thought on the Planet

"So then, do you think that healing is dangerous?" asks Charles. "All the same, once out of danger and healed every ailing person is happy, as are the people related with them."

"Who doesn't feel happy to recover their health, overall, after a long illness? Nevertheless, healing is not without consequence, as every healer takes charge of a potential that can annihilate him. The announcement of their healing to a patient can bring them relief, however the healer takes partial responsibility upon himself for the dangerous future, since the ailing person, satisfied and perhaps cured, does not modify their thoughts or behaviour at all. In the long run, the healer's responsibility can become hellish and even mortal."

"Indeed I know," replies Charles in a surprisingly calm tone of voice. "The official statistics from the assurance companies, that foresee their clients' retirement, are not very comforting for therapists. Life expectancy of these people is shorter and that's why less value is put on them. Your conclusion seems, therefore, logical."

"What do you mean?"

"That healing is dangerous after all."

"It is dangerous only if the healer stops doing therapy. If he ignores the way in which to arrange his potentials, he will find himself faced with new difficulties and will no longer be able to channel them onto his patients. All the time that this transfer of energy potential lasts he lives more or less well. If he eliminates this possibility, what can he do?"

"What do you understand as transfer of energy potential?"

"You can take away the dangerous potential of an ailing person, so they will be healed, but you take charge of this potential. Having the same healer, talking with his patients can open the door to a dangerous potential if you are not protected by your affection and your honesty. Do you know what a *nocebo effect* is?"

"No."

"When we like the updating of a future, we call it a *placebo effect*, when it is damaging, we forget to call it *nocebo*, which in Latin means: to hurt. It is normal to hide what hurts us and keep what we like. There is also a great lack of information about this. Blind experiments have been carried out to test new medicine. Authentic and false medicines are administered to two populations groups who ignore the reality of what they are taking."

"I understand how it works," comments Charles. "The doctor is also in the dark about what he is administering. This way some ill people, without knowing it, take water or sugar. Sometimes they are cured thanks to placebos."

"What has in reality happened is that they have updated an already existent healthy potential. There are other people who suffer secondary effects well before those who take the real medicine. They have found exact information, but this time the updated potential is dangerous and at times mortal. How can such a bad outcome be explained, when this danger still doesn't exist in the population group who took the true medicine? Laboratories call this surprising effect *nocebo* and often hide its existence."

"According to you, is this about a bad collective future or is it that we foolishly extract the information that we need?"

"It's about a bad transfer of energy potential. So that explanation allows us to understand contagion. An epidemic develops quickly as it uses this nocebo effect. A virus or a bacterium that normally isn't harmful can become mortal if its carrier is afraid of falling ill. This fear becomes the cause of his illness, because to open the doors to a dangerous future, it is enough to harbour a thought similar to the one that has created this potential. It is the obligatory relationship between temptation and *sin*, in the Greek sense of this word."

"What can we say about confessors, about the psy...? According to you, with their absolutions or their analysis, do they also take upon themselves the *sins* of their patients, in the Greek sense of the word?"

"Yes! And our political leaders too. Nevertheless, are our political leaders, ignorant of the laws of time, capable of erasing the *sins of the world*? Often, after a hidden consultation with a clairvoyant, they update them, so becoming docile marionettes of a future reality, lost in *the great beyond* of our perceptions of which they are completely unaware."

"Are you serious when you refer to *the great beyond*? Isn't it easier to think that the world is led by a small group of multi-millionaires?"

"And if these multi-millionaires were in the power of our future, which covertly managed them through parasitical information exchanges? Once in place, it is best to inundate the upper part of the pyramid with false information, which will wash down to the lower part. The opposite doesn't work. Nevertheless, leader or led, governor or governed, each one can drink the information from their double that is never filtered through our human hierarchy. He knows that others' future potentials are more dangerous than our own."

"Can we create future potentials adapted to our body and our own problems?"

"Sure, but it is not enough, because we live as a collectivity and we can update an existing future, created by anyone during the 25,000 years of the doubling cycle. As this is now coming to a close, it provides us with a fearful potential. In the future many possibilities have been created that have never been updated to the present. In our time, as we no longer have firewalls which bar the inflexible law of time, humanity is waking up dangerous potentials hidden for millenniums in the darkness of the future. We are disconcerted by the fury of our planet when it is only the result of the updating of catastrophic futures, carried out by each one of us in our daily lives."

"It is difficult, however" adds Charles seriously, "to see the relation between the anger of a man with his wife in spring and the flooding of their house in autumn."

"A violent thought or word unleashes in the future a nocebo effect. Later on, it is enough to update this potential. A small annoyance can also attract a serious consequence already existing in the future. Not to mention the cyclones, tornadoes and tidal waves that can only be unleashed by the violence of a nation! Thoughts are much more destructive than you think. What if we use them in the opposite way? You cannot even imagine their strength. On Reunion Island a river of lava flowed around a church because the faithful liked that meeting place."

"That is a coincidence," concludes my conversation partner who has recovered his *superior intellectual's* prejudices and impatience.

"If the doubles were able to divert a river of lava, why wouldn't they be able to stop a volcanic eruption before the lava flows, the earthquake before the tidal wave, the modification of the axis of the Earth's rotation before the tectonic movements that derive from them, the thaw that modifies this axis, the solar explosions that heat them, etc., etc. Our thoughts modify nature, which is at our service, therefore modifying its potential, so catastrophes are never natural."

Aurelian's father protests. "It is impossible to analyze the future consequences of each one of our thoughts!"

"Only our double can arrange a harmful potential before it can be updated by whomever. On the other hand, according to this same natural process, we can be the creators of the happiness of others without ever seeing anybody."

"You must be kidding!" exclaims Charles staggered. "And besides that, you are going to tell me this with all your personal security and habitual aplomb!"

"So, tell me what I should tell you with my security and habitual aplomb, which is, just so you know, only one of the ways of unleashing intuition."

He doesn't agree. "Intuition! Your personal security can also be simply a pretension and have nothing to do with intuition."

"I never doubt an answer that I still don't know but that probably is on its way, given that you have asked for it. Unleashing intuition can, in fact, give you the feeling of having an answer to everything. Try it yourself and you will be pleased with the result."

"For the moment I prefer to ask you, although with many doubts as to your response. Why does a pleasant thought destroy an unpleasant potential?"

"A pleasant thought towards a person that you pass in the street is enough to unleash a pleasant potential. That person can update a likeable future when their thought is of the same nature. He will immediately feel very happy, without knowing why."

"And what does an unpleasant thought produce?"

"It allows the updating of an unpleasant future that immediately unleashes a defensive reaction. You think, unreasonably, that it is a spontaneous antipathy. Knowledge of this simple mechanism would allow us to resolve most of the problems on Earth. It is not a Utopia, but a law that has become fixed due to the end of the doubling cycle."

"What end?"

"The end of the doubling time. The times, past, present and future, are separated according to the 25,000 year immutable cycles.[1] At the end of this separation, we discover the questions of our doubles and the futures that we have constructed. In the meantime, good or bad, all potentials are accessible. That is why happiness attracts happiness, and the simple fact of considering a small misfortune, attracts the fury from the future."

Charles scoffs. "In other words, so as not to create anything bad in the future you have to be intellectually disabled. If ignorance participates in the disinformation, foolishness does too."

"Not in the future! A simple spirit does not offer a valid thought, only their need for affection. They create an affectionate potential that the intellectual ignores and never updates."

"What would we do in our world with intellectually disabled people in every nook of our streets?"

"We would do marvels in the future. Some African villages, called primitive, embraced them as gods, treating them with great respect. We harass them even in their mothers' womb. Our world rejects the intellectually disabled because we like to *appear.* We are only *bleached tombs* full of putrefaction. We are attracted to the external face of people and we don't know that this attraction can open a door for us to an odious potential. So many people live envying others and don't realise that in this way they destroy themselves! Do you know how a bat finds its way?"

"They are blind animals who send out waves and capture their echo."

"We do the same with the future. We send out questions, but capture other people's answers. It is, therefore, not strange that we

---

1. See: Change your Future through the time Openings.

run into the wall time and again. Without this knowledge of time, science and religion lose their way. There are thousands of millions of potentials hidden in the darkness. As soon as we have a thought similar to one which has already created a future, we can immediately update its consequences; sometimes they are beneficial, but other times they are very dangerous."

"Good or bad, positive or negative" says Charles conclusively, "science and religion look the same."

"Science as well as religion have been constructed upon apparently logical, but not verifiable, postulates and they try to make us survive better or worse. The doubling theory allows people who want provable hypotheses to finally understand that time is divided into past, present and future and that this allows us, amongst other things, to be on the lookout in our daily lives. Nevertheless, this lookout is so quick that we are not conscious of it. Without realising it, we use the moments in which our body submerges us in unconsciousness. There are people who try to consciously look for this state of modified consciousness , through trances, dances, chants, fasts or hypnosis in order to be able to capture what they think to be the future."

"Isn't that what shamans and witchdoctors do?"

"Due to the fact that the doors of the future are wide open, everybody is a shaman or witchdoctor at the end of the doubling time, clairvoyance and foresight are our daily bread. Nowadays the exception would be the person who didn't receive any message from the future. Today Edgar Casey would go unnoticed."

"Are you talking about that clairvoyant who at the beginning of last century surprised the medical world?"

"He spoke of *travelling to a time different from our own* and put himself into a state of auto-hypnosis or unconsciousness to be able to give exact diagnoses and carry out efficient treatments. He also diagnosed ailments and described bacteria that were only known and studied after his death. During his state of trance, almost sleep, he must have made use of the time openings in order to capture information."

"You don't find a guy like that every day!"

"You are mistaken; nowadays we find this type of clairvoyants everywhere. Extensive literature also exists written about *channellers* who are truly in contact with dangerous beings. They are cunningly manipulated so as to, in turn, be able to cunningly manipulate their readers. Nowadays, anybody can access this type of premonitory information."

"Should we run from them?"

"No, they are very useful in case of emergency and the double always goes a second ahead of this parasitic information. There's the example of the dinner guest, invited to some friends' house, who upon hearing radio static thought that a child was being electrocuted. The parents hurried into their daughter's room where she was putting a power point into her mouth. This man, in contact with his double, had divined the danger instinctively."

"I am sure he must have been an electrician!"

"It is not our competency in a subject that gives us the necessary intuition. For example, the surgeon who thanks to our teaching developed control over his intuitions. One day in the street he saw a cyclist, who had just had an accident, lying on the pavement. Without thinking about it twice, he grabbed his knife and cut a hole in the throat of the unfortunate person and was able to save him from dying asphyxiated. His intuition only made his surgical knowledge better."

"Do you want me to believe that anybody can fix a clock, read cards or tea leaves?"

"Only the person who is afraid of these phenomena pushes them away. It's protection. The problem is that nobody knows how to control that which ends up being called paranormal. So, then the person who is marvelled by what they do not understand ends up taking everything as fact and ends up in a sect before having realised that they have become schizophrenic. Who creates better brain washings than the future?"

"And gurus?" adds Charles.

"Like most of the clairvoyants, patented mediums or channellers, a guru is nothing more than the servant of darkness who illuminates it." I tell him as he rummages through a drawer in search of something. "This hellish prophet is still darker than his guides which he mistakes for visionaries. He anticipates the questions that the darkness suggests to him in order to transform us even more into marionettes. And you think what the future wants you to think even before you are aware of what you are thinking. It is easy since anticipation is a vital law ignored by everyone."

You can read the scepticism in Charles' face. "Has this law been proven?"

"There are experiments which demonstrate this perfectly[2], thanks to diagnosis through images, which make use of the undulatory technique: ultrasound, brain, and CAT scans as well as other means. Nevertheless, classical medicine scorns the influence of the waves that our body receives. Nowadays, it is possible to visualise the part of the brain that is activated only by the will of carrying out a concrete gesture."

"And?"

"Having this located, anticipation has been able to be demonstrated. You decide to raise your arm because your neurons have

_____

2. Benjamin Libet's experiments show the average time of anticipation to be between 0.4 and 0.7 seconds. These experiments were confirmed in 2005 by medical diagnostic imaging.

already decided that you do it even before you become conscious of it. The only problem is knowing if it is you who orders your brain or another person. Just so you know, the act of raising an arm is not insipid, you could be grabbing onto an odious potential."

"How is that?"

"Think of all those who have raised their arm saying *Heil Hitler!* Because of this simple gesture, they have been partially responsible for millions of deaths."

"You exaggerate a little!" says Charles who, nevertheless, with great shock begins to realise the big responsibility that each one of us has. "What do you say then about those who make the sign of the cross?"

"These people can update the potentials created by generations of superstitious people and think that this is the way to make their desires reach God's ears."

With a satisfied smile, Charles takes a pendulum out of the drawer. His happiness seems to be that of a child who has been caught with their hand inside the jar of preserves.

"Let's see who bosses who. You've just told me that my brain receives information even before I realise it." To his amazement the pendulum begins to spin rapidly. "You see the pendulum spins without me thinking anything," he says believing to have the explanation of this phenomenon well-known to adepts of divination.

"No. What you believe is that you aren't thinking anything, but in reality you want to demonstrate to yourself that it spins without you thinking anything and the future immediately demonstrates that this potential exists. Millions of people make their pendulums spin to prove that what they think is true."

"So what's dangerous about that?"

"With knowledge of anticipation, it can be said that you receive information from the future before even being conscious of it. Nevertheless, you are the one who has attracted it because the beginning of your thought has made individual or collective past projects resurface. These have unleashed a potential and your brain updates this future before you have time to finish your thought. The immediate need to move the pendulum comes to you in the guise of instinct or simply a reflection. What has happened is that you have simply updated an existing future through a time opening before even having known it."

"Do you really think that I act like that upon matter?" he says looking at how the pendulum moves.

"Animals do it for their well-being. Have you heard of *psycho kinesis*? For them this is natural, they know how to use a reality from another time."

"Do you, a man of science, believe in psycho kinesis?" he says with great surprise as he puts away his pendulum."

"It is totally scientific. For example, when a chick comes out of his shell, whatever moves, becomes his mother. This has also been scientifically demonstrated.[3] For example, in the moment previous to the egg hatching, place a small vehicle in front of it which moves about randomly, you will see something surprising: its trajectory will no longer be random as it will come closer to the chick. In the same way, if you place a vehicle which is scary due to its colour or sound, it will move away from the chick."

"You don't mean to say that the animal modifies the behaviour of a machine?"

"Of course I do! It is true that everyone thinks that a vehicle doesn't have a soul, but another series of experiments proves this reality, meaning to say, the influence of animal thought upon matter. A mouse is placed at the entrance of a labyrinth whose

_____

3. Lorenz imprinting.

passageways have all, but one, been conveniently electrified. Divining the unpredictable, the mouse almost always takes the pathway free from electrical discharges in search of food at the other extreme."

"I don't question these experiments, I know that they are true, but we are not mice!"

"Anticipation has to do with all the animals, including ourselves. A machine is only a heap of particles in movement, like us. The mouse proves to us that it is an excellent physicist of particles. Your computer confounds your behaviour which in turn confounds it. If the micro-wave oven is capable of transforming the vital information of our food to the point of misinforming us, the opposite is also possible. Who has not observed the influence of man on vegetation? Some of us make plants grow marvellously."

"You mean to say that they *have green fingers*?"

"Good attention updates the best future. Plants benefit from it. In the same way, we could give healthy information to food before eating it or to machines before using them. The blessing of food before eating by the Catholics would therefore have a justification. Knowing this, we should associate a thought with each one of our gestures."

"Just what we were missing!" exclaims Charles, "with the electrical networks, power points, radios, telephones and all that mess of undulatory information, your anticipative information must not be very reliable."

"Dreams and times called *unconsciousness* always take us on long necessary trips, where we find the best balance possible. Always known, much stronger than the atom bomb, the blistering acceleration of time gives us great strength at every instant. Without knowing it, we make use of this time bomb in our daily lives. We unleash it every time we want to. We waste our energy thinking bad thoughts and so weaken our survival potential which will be necessary for us after our death."

"This is all fine and good and I don't tire of listening to you" says Charles, "but any sensible man will tell you that if it were true, it would be known."

"That is what the sceptics say who leave us perplexed by their ignorance. How many people would still be using candle light if we hadn't accepted the reality of electricity? All that is vital is known naturally. We don't need teachings in order to survive! Animals demonstrate this to us through a multitude of examples in daily life that we no longer know how to decipher. A horse stops as soon as it feels danger, but his rider, who disregards this and spurs him on, will have to face the danger that his mount wanted him to avoid."

Surprised, Charles adds "In fact, the elephants broke their chains and escaped from the area before the tsunami."

"In the same way, fish, warned of the danger, fled from the earthquake and saved the lives of the fishermen who followed them. They found only a few rat cadavers when there had been millions of rats. In the past, everyone knew that they abandoned a ship beforehand in the harbour, foreseeing a storm that would sink it in high seas. Why are we not capable of imitating animals? We should have it clear that those who create our future are those that take advantage of our ignorance!"

20
Information Exchanges

A satisfied smile lights up Aurelian's face, who, sitting comfortably in his chair, has not at any point lost the thread of the conversation. "If during our sleep, we exchange our energetic bodies with those of our double, it has nothing to do with our future, does it?"

"That is a first exchange, but this other *me* doesn't stay there. His energetic body continues its voyage towards our future in search of answers that correspond to his questions, but he only finds them if we have already created them with our thoughts. Meanwhile an energetic body from the future substitutes ours."

"Why?"

"To keep us alive. He offers his own questions and his own answers. Without the control of our double, this could be contrary to our concerns and would give us false information, inadapted to our body, which could see itself seriously mistreated."

"Does that mean that my body is at the mercy of the future?" Aurelian asks uneasily, apparently astonished by this idea.

"No. No energy from the future is master of our time. That is why during the exchange our body cannot move. Nevertheless, it warehouses information from the future. This explains our immobility, called postural atony, and the intense intellectual activity that makes our eyes move in all directions. Upon waking up, you accept new ideas, only if you like them mentally, as well as physically. In reality, you become clairvoyant without knowing it. If your double never intervenes, you could wake up tense or depressed, because you run the risk of thinking things that are unacceptable to your body or spirit."

"That's not possible. I've already told you that I rarely remember my dreams!"

"But your body does remember them and gives you information that can be odious. Besides that, as the future is a different reality from our own, it is difficult to understand our dreams. It is better to leave our problems with our double, so that he can arrange them, since the future has the same reality as his; accelerated, he sees all the possibilities that we have slowly passing by. Thanks to our double, from the next day forward we can update the best potential. Don't forget that thousands of millions of time openings exist during paradoxical dreams. Your double can resolve thousands of millions of problems. Making this exchange with him is the only way to live without worries and overall, without fear of tomorrow. If not, you cannot control the future. You fill yourself with strange thoughts that parasitize you and impel you to do things that normally you would never have felt like doing."

"Why wouldn't the future give me the right information?"

"It's as if you ask a passer-by who thinks he knows the way. Would he give you the right indications? The future is full of liars who live according to our thoughts."

"By the way, you still haven't explained to me how to get rid of those troublemakers. Do you remember?"

"It is enough for you to live in affection and honesty. As Jesus said, it is your only protection against the hells where the Prince of Darkness reigns. God of the Shadows of the Sumerians, demons of the infernal regions, these dark worlds analyze our thoughts to create their consequences. They do nothing more than create the life that we desire.

Our questions allow them to create their answers. If they want to live as they please, they modify them. Nightmares are no more than the consequence of these uncontrolled exchanges. This is the way that little by little our personality changes and without realising it we enter into the kingdom of schizophrenics."

"What's a schizophrenic?"

"It is a person who feels so attracted to the future that the future is with them practically all the time. Their personality is double because their double is no longer ever with them. Little by little they get used to the darkness."

"Why doesn't anybody talk to us about this double?" asks Aurelian at the same time that he looks at his mother who has just come into the sitting room.

"He is not a complete stranger. Some see in him a guide or an angel who evolves in a mysterious world."

"Other people" his mother adds "prefer to believe that an innate consciousness or a collective unconsciousness, related to the past or to evolutionary coincidence, drags us towards oblivion or eternal rest."

"Good luck or bad, God or devil, co-incidence or pre-destination, everybody is right, nobody is guilty, because this other *self* is our relationship to immortality: a creative piece of a time different from our own. In the *great beyond* of our habitual perceptions, there is a perfectly real invisibility, so to say."

"Then we should be able to become familiar with it," replies the child.

"It is too dangerous; the light of its slowed-down time would kill us. We pass each other in our exchanges, but we never see each other. Sometimes when your double comes to you at night and sees your horrible futures, he doesn't dare and you become a sleep-walker."

Aurelian, nervous, stares at me. "But I'm a sleeee-pwa-lker..." he stutters. "Aren't I, Mum?"

"Aurelian has just come through a sleepwalking crisis," his mother confirms, suddenly feeling uncomfortable.

"It is a common occurrence at his age, as a child tries to fly with his own wings far from his double. It can turn dramatic during puberty, as we suddenly deviate from the path that we have marked since before being born. Our double feels so disgruntled that he tries to demonstrate it by giving us a shake up."

"Do you mean to say that I have a rotten future ahead of me?" Aurelian asks nervously, "That's it, isn't it?"

I sooth him. "All of us are on Earth because our future is more or less rotten. Do not forget that we have done many things in our space since 25,000 years ago. Sleepwalking is not a punishment! In the past the entire tribe would have asked you questions to listen to the gods within you. Nowadays, we prefer to prescribe pills that suppress sleepwalking as well as the information from you double."

"Yesterday I sleep well, but..." he says after reflecting "it was the future that was inside me, he was the one who slept well."

"He doesn't sleep inside you, but only takes knowledge of your questions and of your worries that will modify his behaviour and his thoughts later on in his reality. It is an exchange: your thoughts change the future, which changes your thoughts."

Aurelian looked at his mother with a smile. "That is when our bad cells commit suicide!"

His mother shrugs her shoulders and gently chides her son. "Don't talk foolishness!"

"He's right," I tell her, "a sole night can be enough to put us back in shape. This quickly recovered balance, sometimes instantaneously, gives the impression of sudden balance, miraculous. It's a question of updating in our body a potential already existent in our future."

"If my double comes to me, can I meet up with him?"

"No, only death can re-unite us."

"Nevertheless, there are many people who see in a luminous being in dreams," exclaims his mother. "Are those people guided by their doubles?"

"No, they are only gullible prey of the gods of the shadows who dazzle them with their lies. Only our doubles are beings of light and we will be able to see ours only after our death. Sometimes, when there is an emergency, a luminous vibration can let us know of their presence. Why would he waste energy like that if not warn us that he needs answers to one of his questions? For example, to announce a birth, or a death, some news or a necessary turn in our lives. In all of these cases and as we are coming to the end of a doubling cycle, it is necessary to use our double to be sure of not confusing ourselves by our guide or direction."

Aurelian adds "So with him, I should be able to immediately obtain everything that I desire for my future, right?"

"No, as there exists a gap of forty days between the instant in which we desire a future and the moment in which we can update it. This time lapse has its explanation."

"What a drag!"

"No, it's for safety. Think! Only one of your thoughts instantaneously creates the corresponding future. Somebody can update that potential by only having a similar thought. If you want to avoid that responsibility, you have forty days to change that future with your double's help. It is the same principle as the forty days of Lent."

"But if I need a future immediately for my survival, what do I do? I'm not going to wait all that time."

"There are thousands and thousands of millions of available potentials in the entire world; you can find one that is adapted to your case."

"Are you talking about collective unconsciousness?" asked Francoise.

"The unconscious is in reality a memorisable conscience, but in moments so quick that it always appears to be outside of our consciousness. Nevertheless, it modifies our present instantaneously. You have at your disposal, every instant, information which arrives so quickly that it is presented in the form of intuition, suggestion or foresight. The problem is to know how to distinguish the information of our double from that of the future."

"And how do we do that?" asks the child.

"We have to understand that nothing good comes out of the darkness. Are you afraid of the dark?"

"Yes, of course."

"That's normal! Children are always afraid of the bad exchanges that take place in the darkness of accelerated time. When they wake up and talk about their fear, their parents try to resolve the situation by putting a small night light in their bedroom. This calms the baby, but as he is unaware that his fear attracts a future capable of giving him still more fear, he will be even more inclined to having nightmares; he'll receive information that his body won't accept. This will bring about physical problems, the most benign being nappy rash, eczema, allergies...the most virulent could bring about death called SIDS, sudden infant death syndrome."

"Do you hear that, Mum?" Aurelian asks his mother.

"Son, you should let Jean-Pierre leave, unless you can stay a little longer," she says looking at me. "What you are saying is so good for us all!"

"Why don't you tell all the kids that there isn't any reason to be afraid of the dark?" Aurelian asks me.

"It isn't possible to explain to a child, a few days or months or years old, the doubling theory and what it implies in our daily lives." I turn towards his mother, "Anyway nothing is left up to chance. The doubles of children and their mothers serve as a common communication channel of information, allowing them to be counselled at the same time. This way the child can be calmed by her mother if she understands that the number one reason for her child's night-mares is anguish."

"In fact, I have realised that my son communicated his fears to me, but the opposite also occurred."

The child looks at his mother perplexed. "But I am not afraid of you!"

"Nevertheless, it is true." I say. "So many mothers transmit their anxiety! *I was like him, I was afraid of the dark.* A mother will tell us; not knowing that the future will prove her way of thinking right. On the other hand, if you understand that darkness only brings about the consequences of the thoughts that you have attributed to it, the child will no longer need a light in order to go to sleep."

"Then, Mum has done it all backwards and I have too!" cries Aure-lian. "She doesn't know that I feel her sadness and I don't know that her tears are mine. Dad doesn't know that the dark shadows I see around my bed at night are real either. Every time I talk about it, he says: *When you're older you, will laugh about it, like me, you won't be afraid of anything anymore.* One day I answered him: *When you die, you'll see the bad people around you and then you won't be laughing so much. And there won't even be police to go complain to.*"

"What did he say?"

Aurelian hesitates to answer. "My husband doesn't like to be contradicted," answers his mother turning towards me. "What can you do so that a child isn't afraid of the darkness anymore?"

"You can tell him a story before he falls asleep. The action of turning off the light without fearing that he feels bad is enough for his phobia of the darkness to disappear. Of course, we should get used to doing it like that from the moment he is born, as the child feels the strong physical presence of his mother as a vital source of information.

A separation can provoke a indescribable fear, often expressed in wailing, which even a very talented father cannot dissipate." A recent example comes to mind and I tell it to them.

"A mother had just been told that they couldn't do anything for her three-year-old son. He had terrible pains and the doctors had diagnosed cancer of the spinal column in terminal phase. The mother was broken by pain and anguish. A friend of hers spoke to her of our knowledge and she called us."

"What can you say to a mother on tranquilisers and a son on morphine? In strong doses, drugs perturb paradoxical sleep as well as the healthy information exchanges with the double."

"We suggested, if possible, stopping the ingestion of sedatives one or two hours that same night, on the condition of taking them again if she felt bad. Watch out! We were talking about sedatives and not medicine. The suppression of a medicine is serious and can set off a still graver potential. It is too dangerous to take on this responsibility. In this concrete case, the provoked pain and anguish, being efficient alarm bells, can only touch off the desire to appease them. It is not harmful to leave the sedative close at hand."

"And what can you do with a small child who cannot understand the mechanism of information exchanges with his double or the efficiency of controlling his way of falling asleep?"

"Don't tell me that telling him a story is enough!" cries Aurelian, sceptically.

"Not exactly! If the mother knows how to squash her anguish and if she is certain that her double is going to resolve everything, it is clear that the next day will offer the absolute best. But careful! We advise telling improvised tales, not all those that are told everywhere and that can bring about a relapse into dangerous potentials."

"It is easy to tell any kind of story, if you listen carefully to the words that come into your head. We discover the story at the same time as we're telling it. The child falls asleep even before we arrive to the end. In this mother's case, her surprise was even greater as the two fell asleep before telling the end of the tale. And the best part is that both of them woke up ten hours later completely at peace and soothed."

"You see" exclaims Aurelian, annoyed and critical, "tonight you are coming to tuck me in and tell me Tom Thumb, revised and corrected by your double. I suck my thumb and everything's great!

"Why do you think that your double can't tell you an age-appropriate story? I thought that you had understood the colossal force of his information. With the common channel of a mother and child, it appears almost miraculous; however there is nothing abnormal or paranormal about it. It is enough to know how to extract information from an existing potential which corresponds to the needs of our body and that, only our double can do."

Aurelian raises his eyes to the sky. "Don't get angry. I said something stupid. You don't have to make it into a scary movie!"

21

The Role of the Mother

"The role of the mother is fundamental, as the information exchange is permanent between her and her children."

Worried by this new information, Francoise asks "What do you mean?"

"Every pregnant woman knows that her thoughts change. What she doesn't know is that this change is brought about by the double of the child she is carrying. She receives information destined for the foetus that she takes for new and brilliant intuitions, because they are often different from hers. This explains the inexplicable cravings that pregnant women have."

"Do you think that ceases after giving birth?"

"The physical craving, yes, but the information exchanges between the mother and her child are permanent. They are very strong until the child reaches the age of seven. In primitive tribes it was at the end of this important period when the child was given their adult name as they were entering into the age of reason."

"My grandmother doesn't even know who or where she is any more. Will my mother become like her, because she's her daughter?"

"That is another subject," says his mother, "it's an illness called Alzheimer's."

"You, who are her daughter, can ask your double the reason behind this loss of memory. The information channel between mother and daughter is the same throughout their lives and even after death. Jewish people consider that a child is Jewish only if their mother is. To my way of thinking this is a miserly, but human, precaution, as the husband isn't necessarily the biological father of the child. But his concern was about something else."

"What?"

"Live or dead, the mother transmits information originally from her double, equally to her children as to her own mother. This indelible relationship, through successive generations, provides a determined objective to a nation, century after century. The Egyptians knew it and the Jews, who had been their slaves, knew it too."

"And me," says Aurelian leaving the room, "I am a slave to my body who must evacuate bad information."

His mother smiles at the same time she asks me "You mean to say that I can help my mother by the simple fact of being her daughter?"

"Maternal lineage provides immediate information from mother to child as well as from child to mother during their entire lives. It is true that at times this common channel is not always equally as efficient. It follows a cycle of seven years: the age of reason, puberty, etc...The cells in our body also follow this cycle since they are totally renewed every seven years. That is why it's important to inform the new cells, so that they live the new cycle without any problems. So many ailments are triggered in just these moments! The relationship between mother and child is always healthy as long as the information channel with their double is not cut."

"If there is a problem, can this channel be shut?"

"It is easily opened as soon as affection comes into play. The balance or imbalance of one of the two brings about the balance or imbalance of the other. External or bodily manifestations don't have to be the same."

An example comes to mind. "A baby had a purulent eczema. Her mother blamed the baby's formula. The father, a believer in natural remedies, went from farm to farm looking for mare's milk, but that didn't help either! Their only reward was exhaustion and insomnia. One sole control of the way they fell asleep was enough for the anguish to disappear. A few nights later, to their great surprise, the eczema had completely disappeared."

"Nobody knows that a child captures the anguish or happiness of their mother through the channel that they have in common. A child sees the potentials that fill their nights with violent nightmares or marvellous dreams which make them smile like a cherub, as was said in olden times. When there is no happiness at home, the child can update the potentials of the mother and moan without apparent cause."

"Are you sure you don't want to stay a little while longer? Charles and I would be delighted if you stayed to have lunch with us." Francoise says, looking at my wife.

"You can see that he doesn't want to," Aurelian sighs, "he has to go visit other people, more important than us."

"If you predict lies to find out the truth, the future immediately arranges itself so that the truth is a consequence of the falsehood that you imagine and you become entangled. I promise to come back tomorrow."

"If I am unable to sleep like I should," Aurelian says, "it'll be your fault."

"For tonight, ask your mother for help!"

"What do I have to do?" his mother asks.

"He already told you!" her son shouts, "tell me a bedtime story."

I turn towards Francoise, "Or simply tell your double Aurelian's story, because perhaps he doesn't tell it right himself!"

Faced with the family's insistence, we could not turn down the invitation. Aurelian's happiness was a pleasure to behold. He raised his arm very high in a quick gesture, making the sign of victory. He had won!

22

Once upon a time, there will be...

We could live so many pleasant moments if we knew how to create and update the marvellous tales of the future!

"What are the tales of the future? Come on, tell them to us!"

"I can tell you one, if you wish."

"I am listening" Aurelian answers enthusiastically.

"Once upon a time, there will be..." I say plagiarising the tales, "a woman who leaves her house every morning to go to work, turning right on Monotony Street. One morning she turns left onto Happiness Street. A little further ahead, a driver cannot start up his car. He will never know that this momentary break down will keep him from driving off until the love of his life reaches him. Lost in her thoughts, the woman comes towards a marvellous destiny which she is unaware of. All of a sudden she stops and realises she is disoriented and angry with herself, she quickly turns around. The driver is then able to start his car. The fairly tales ends there, because the woman will never know that her disorientation was not fortuitous, just like the curious break down of the pretty car of the handsome gentleman, Prince Charming, as loving in the future as he is indifferent to the charms of this woman in the present. *She will not be happy and won't have seven children in a beautiful medieval castle where she will not live.*"

"I don't like your story!" Aurelian chimes in. "How can she know that she has walked past a lovely fairy tale?"

"The day that she visits that castle, together with her husband who has never filled her with happiness, she will have the sensation of having lived there because she will have in her memory this lovely potential which has never been updated. Perhaps she will see a hypnotist who will bring to light this story of the future, thinking that it is a past life. Afterwards she will try to understand something of this story, something that is impossible to understand without the explanation that I am giving you."

"And if the woman had not turned around," Aurelian adds, looking at his mother, "maybe she would have run into bad people, armed to the teeth, instead of Prince Charming! She'll be scared out of her wits and will never be able to sing again nor play the violin, which she will love to do when she is old. Overall, if she has a mother who sends her to see a hypnotist, who tries to figure out something dark that is impossible to understand in that way."

There is no need to be a clairvoyant to know that this child is speaking for his mother, who looks at me uneasily. I know, that in few words, Aurelian has just told us a part of his big problem. I am perplexed.

"If you are used to being in contact with your double, you don't risk any danger. It is enough to be confident. A good-looking young woman, coming back home in the early hours wearing a provocative dress, can pass right through a gang of troublemakers without being afraid. If she disposes of a good potential, she will go by without any problem. The only difficulty is to not doubt and maintain her affection."

"Feel affection in the middle of troublemakers, you must be joking. Besides that, they can attack you all of a sudden, without you seeing it coming."

Francoise interrupts him. "Aurelian, please," she says. "Do his questions bother you?" she asks me confused.

I shake my head to let her know everything is fine and I go ahead.

"If you have a good potential ahead of you, you don't have anything to be afraid of. It depends upon you to create it ahead of time. Affection will always be your protection."

"Affection when you're dying of fright, what a line!" protests the child.

"You shouldn't send bad thoughts to troublemakers, that is affection! Otherwise you activate their violence, as well as your fear, which pushes your double away. Take for example the child who after having fallen from a fifth floor flat, gets up smiling, with just a few scratches. His parents were dumbfounded. Why?"

"Because he bounced!" Aurelian bends over laughing.

"Not exactly! He's intact because he doesn't know that he can die. He even likes to fly sucking his thumb. He is totally confident and accepts the solution, which he is unaware of. That way he doesn't update anything bad among the available futures. That is how he attracts his double to him and the exchange of the energetic bodies brings about such a strong levitation that he doesn't hurt himself at all."

Francoise seems surprised. "Do you believe in levitation?" she asks.

How do I explain in a few words what has taken me 15 years to understand? To speak of levitation now would be out of place to me. We would have to talk about anti-gravitational energy and so many other things that have to do with time and doubling, that standing before this child I don't feel capable of.

23

The Sign of Jonah

"You write that you have had an exceptional encounter and a life turned around," Aurelian says, who, with my book on his knees, reads in his small voice, slowly but securely. "*On the night of 21 October 1988, I had the sudden sensation that time was stopping. Amazing information invaded me...*Tell me, where did this information come to you from?"

"From my double! Only at that time, I was totally unaware of his existence."

"Have you seen him?"

"No."

"Too much for the body!"

"You know, overall, I felt a sense of urgency, as if our ignorance were dragging us towards a large-scale cataclysm. Besides that, I understood that we are living the end of an important solar cycle, that I had to understand this well to be able to explain it to others, so that each and every person could sooth this planet. It is about time, since the sign of Jonah is there and nobody sees it!"

"What is the sign of Jonah?"

"It is the sign transmitted to humanity at the end of the doubling time. It is found there, in the sky."

"Whereabouts?"

"Our planets form a kind of luminous disk and around them an enormous dark light turns, which we call the Oort cloud. Look at this photograph," I tell Aurelian, "it is the image of a star at the end of its cycle."

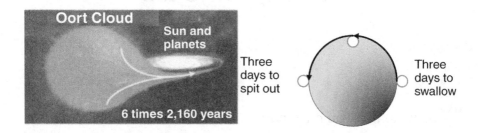

This image is, in reality, that of another solar system.

"A doubling cycle lasts 25,000 years. It is broken up into twelve periods of 2,070 years. In former times they talked about the six days and six nights that made up the week of creation, before the Lord's day of rest. It is written in the book that you have in your hands. This corresponds to the cycle well-known to the astrophysicists of 25,920 years. During the first three *days*, the cloud aspirates the planetary disk and during the last three, it spits everything out. Pedagogically we can say, as our ancestors said, that the whale swallowed the little fish so as to spit it out on the banks of the other world three days later. In Greek Jonah means *he that is*, which is to say he that becomes real upon leaving the darkness. He is still violet, which is said *Jon*. Since three years ago, near Pluto, enormous planetoids can be observed, as big as this last planet of our solar system. Imagine the commotion that that can bring about on the gravitational balance of our group of planets. The forces in action are equal to thousands of millions of atomic bombs. And this doesn't appear to interest anyone...at least not officially!"

"And you think that you are going to wake up the world?" Aurelian says with relevance, both uneasy and sceptical.

"That is my goal! Taking consciousness from the strength of our double, we can change our potentials and attract the best future for ourselves. We may still have a few years..."

"Ah!" exclaims the child, "*We've gotta get on it*, as my dad says."

"The Gospels tell us: *And when ye shall see Jerusalem compassed with armies, then know that the desolation thereof is nigh. And there shall be signs in the sun, and the moon, and in the stars...for the powers of heaven shall be shaken.*[1] Do you know what I think of this?"

"No."

"It will be more difficult to bring peace to Israel than to any other nation."

"Why is that?"

"Two thousand years ago, before the last *night*, there was born in Israel a Jewish Palestinian Christian called Yeshua. The Prince of Light had attracted the Prince of Darkness...and like now, light illuminates the dawn of the *seventh day*, darkness invades us where the big light had appeared to us. Each one of us needs to light our lanterns!"

---

1. The Gospel According to Saint Luke: 21, 20-26.

24

Inspiration and Creativity

As soon as the meal has finished, Aurelian gets up, throwing his hands to his head. "But Dad, you have forgotten our rehearsal! Octavia is going to be here and I won't have begun. She's coming over again to give me a kiss."

He turns towards me as if he were irritated. "You know, she always wipes her mouth before and after giving me a kiss? That bothers me a lot! She's lucky that I love her!"

He runs out and quickly comes back with his violin and sheet music. Charles, annoyed, asks that we excuse him and briefly explains that he can't put off this moment that his son is so looking forward to. I follow them to the sitting room. Charles heads towards the piano and Aurelian follows him. Together they start to play with great virtuosity.

I feel marvelled and touched by this young violinist and end up discovering tears on his cheeks. Does he truly feel so moved to play for me? Is this the way he demonstrates a great artistic talent? He stops playing all of a sudden and leaves the room.

Charles gets up from the piano uneasily and again begs our pardon, explaining the reason for this incident. His son, having to play in public, once again realises that he is not at this best.

"He loses confidence in himself and this irritates him. He's so worried about other things!"

A few minutes later, his eyes dried, Aurelian comes back. He throws himself upon me, his eyes suddenly shining with a gleam that expresses a sudden hope, as if he has just realised that I can be his saviour.

"Now, it's your turn!" he tells me with a decided air.

I look at him in surprise, fearful of disappointing him. He starts laughing as he guesses my apprehension.

"I am not asking you to play, but to help me to play!"

Charles carries on, half serious, half joking. "Haven't you said before that, like a bird in its nest, a child builds his future from the very moment of birth? So, without thinking about it, with the help of a fairy that doubles him, bent over the cot, he will find the bow and the violin and all the inspiration to be able to play upon Earth. Why not think that the well-meaning fairy could come to our aid? I am also counting on you, this is very important."

Without waiting for my answer, he sits down in front of the piano while Aurelian looks at me with the trust and certainty that I cannot disappoint. What else can I do if not ask for urgent help from that double whom I talk so much about. I silently implore him.

"Do not leave us aside! Find the best solution for this child so full of confidence!"

The concert, and it was a concert, surpassed anything that Charles and Aurelian could have expected. Once finished, they began a beautiful improvisation. The emotion was so great that Charles cried like a child while his son smiled at me with an endearing look.

On tiptoe, Francoise, Lucile and a small girl entered the sitting room and sat down behind Aurelian. It seemed to me that this lovely blonde doll was Octavia. The same grave face as the boy, surrounded by curly hair, seemed to irradiate curiosity mixed with impatience.

The next quarter of an hour was marvellous, extra-ordinary.

Aurelian came to thank me with a noisy kiss on each cheek, but I push him gently away.

"How have you done that?" he says happily.

"I don't have anything to do with that, you know. Give thanks to your double! He is the good fairy who bent over your cot to give you this uncommon gift."

Charles looks at his hands, amazed. "This is incredible! My hands seemed to play independently from me. I saw them play, as if I were outside of myself, at the same time as being here."

"How lovely!" Octavia exclaims, still under the effects of the music. She gives a kiss to Aurelian, this time forgetting to wipe her lips before and afterwards. Aurelian is so happy that he starts to play a folkloric melody based on a mixture of French Auvernian dance music and American country. His father accompanies him on piano with a mad and happy complicity.

A bit of coffee restores our equanimity while Aurelian and Octavia go out for a walk.

"What do you think has happened?" Charles asks, still under the effects of amazement. Is it possible that I have updated, like you say, a marvellous music, because it has truly been divine!"

"This updating has been inspired by the doubles. Our epoch can offer us great pleasures because it puts us in contact with our greatest potentials. Unfortunately, through ignorance and due to our thoughts, we only update the worst."

"Are you talking about the informants from the future?"

"They are always pendant on our information. If our desires and our projects are wonderful, we attract the best and expulse the worst. We have just experimented proof of this. All of our cells have felt intensely emotional. Anyway, the end of our time will not give us the advantage of modifying our future at every instant. The reality that we have considered indifferently on Earth during centuries will

become ours. It is better for the creatures from the future to not mani-
fest themselves beforehand. They are only our musicians who try to
pass themselves off as orchestra conductors so that we might play
their composition." Seeing his doubtful gesture, I become impatient
and try to anticipate his re-action taking a short cut. "And there will
always be some fool who says: *if there were the great beyond, its
inhabitants would have let themselves be known a long time ago.
No dead person has ever come back to confirm this.*"

"I agree with you. That way of thinking is silly!"

"Beings, whom doubling hides in our darkness, know us very well,
since they have transformed us and continue to do so as much as
they can, at the same time that they maintain themselves invisible
behind the doors of our dreams. We are schizophrenic marionettes
who are happy to be so."

"Aren't you a little pessimistic?"

"On the contrary, you have seen that there exists means of being
very optimistic. I only wish that there be a great number of people
on Earth who know so, before it is too late. The end of doubling time
approaches to us also from the past and therefore from the saving
creative substance. In Greek, to be next *para* to this substance
ousia is said *parousia*, which means immediate balance. In reality,
it is only since March of 1989, the date of the solar explosion which
we have spoken about earlier, that this *apocalyptic Paraousia* is
possible for each one of us. Your concert has taken strength from
this magnificent energy."

A concealed surprise is read in Charles' face. "If I have understood
correctly, everything is in the hands of this famous double! Do you
think that he could have played instead of me?"

"He has contributed to your playing."

"I am not so sure about that," he proclaims. "It is true that during
an improvisation I don't know where my fingers go and I don't think

about anything concretely. But it is also true that I have acquired technique and my hands are the ones that play."

"Our competence in our reality is a plus but it is not indispensable in case of an emergency. One day, on a straightaway, our car began to spin around like a top. I saw myself drive as if I were a Formula One champion, when I have never in my life participated in any sort of car race, nor have I ever learned to manage a car when it's spinning around at high speed. It was impressive. What do you think of that?"

"I think," Francoise intervened more confidently than her husband, "that that must also be possible at the piano!"

"When you decide not to decide anything else," I tell her, "you are no longer the creator and your double comes to create in your place. Then it is normal to feel safe in the car and divine at the piano. It works the same way to bring about intuitions and foresight. There is nothing simpler, so much so that everyone considers it too simple and doesn't try to find out for themselves how easy it is."

"I think that to make good use of our double, we must go back to being children with absolute trust and each day ask that other part of us: *Thy will be done!*"

"The only thing about all our stories that makes me sad," Charles concludes smiling, "is that, once again, my wife is right." With certain humility, he draws close to her and puts his hand on her shoulder.

25

The existence of God is certainty, faith is an error in uncertainty

We had created bonds with this family and it was difficult for us to refuse their dinner invitation. After giving everyone a kiss, Aurelian retired to do his homework. After dinner, in their son's absence, we think his parents will speak to us more openly.

I decide to ask a crucial question. "The first day, Aurelian told me that his mother had a big problem."

"The big problem is him." Francoise says.

I feel she is relieved.

"My son no longer wants to go to school," Charles says looking at us unwaveringly. "There are some troublemakers who have been attacking him and robbing him in the last few months. We don't know who they are. But since three days ago, his fear seems to be neutralised, his nightmares too, and his sleep walking has stopped. He isn't as tense as before and is even going to school alone and none of us are taking tranquillisers now as for some reason we are no longer anguished. Nevertheless, we don't dare speak of it for fear that he'll fall ill again and vomit all his food."

"Give thanks to your doubles. They only await this from us to feel better and accelerate beneficial changes."

Charles appears fed up. "But I haven't asked for anything! Why do you want me to give thanks to this other, completely hypothetical *I* when I know that I am here alone and unable to help my son?"

"As you said, I have asked my double to find the best solution to this problem," Francoise comments humbly, which draws a great sigh from her husband.

"And I am waiting to see to believe," Charles adds drily. "Why do people always want to explain the inexplicable, if it's about God or a double? I don't believe in God and besides that, I am proud of it."

"I don't believe in God either."

Charles is amazed. "You don't believe in God?"

Open-mouthed and staggered, he throws a glance at his wife, who as surprised as him, questions us with her eyes.

"There is no need to believe, as it is certainty," specifies my wife, Lucile. "For me, it is clear that one plus one is two, but I am not able to demonstrate it and it is very difficult to do so. Only competent mathematicians have been able to. I want to believe them, but I don't think that one and one is equal to two, but I am sure of it because thanks to these mathematicians, it is trustworthy. In order to go more quickly, try going down stairs four at a time, thinking that one plus one is five and you will see the outcome in hospital!"

"But the existence of God cannot be demonstrated," protests Charles, who has recovered his condescending tone of voice of the superior intellectual.

"Of course it can!" I say firmly. "A creation needs a sole creator in another time. This is not dogma, but a physical law. We are creatures well-made to know that we are not unique. Our present time is found in the future of the Creator whose present is a rigorously demonstrable reality." Before Charles comes out with one of his favourite argument, I add, "In reality the doubling theory highlights the law of the alpha and the omega that is as old as time. For the Sumerians, seven places separated the On High from the One Below. There were seven divine laws which united them and seven doors to pass through. Where do you think that this knowledge came from? They also had their astrophysicists, who were called wizards!"

"Our material technologies, which have nothing to do with their insignificant arms, come from rigorously exact laws," exclaims Charles, who is starting to get nervous. "Where is the technology of your Sumerians?"

I quickly answer him. "It is not because everything works that we must deduce that the physical law, which proves that everything works, is exact. To say that the cipher π is an exact number[1], when it isn't, under the pretext that a wheel turns perfectly, is an error. The law that measures that circle is not exact, but the circle is!"

"Previously, faith did not exist," Lucile adds. "Do you know that the word *faith*, in the sense that we understand it today, does not exist in the Bible, written in Greek, which has arrived to us? That is a bad translation of the word *pistis,* which means *a demonstrable way of inspiring confidence*, meaning trustworthy. So in the Gospels, an ailing woman is happy to touch Jesus' clothing, who in that time would have said to her: *Go in peace, your faith has saved you.* Which for her, as well as for him, makes no sense. Nevertheless, to say *your certainty* or *your trustworthy confidence has saved* you is normal, since certainty instantaneously updates the corresponding potential."

I add, "With the word *pistis*, there would be no misunderstanding. For example, when asking for a loan, the banker required a *pistis* from his client as a guarantee. Nowadays, it would be difficult to imagine a banker accepting a large overdraft from his client in *faith* or because of their pretty face!"

"Mine would," Charles quickly responds.

---

1. A circle of radius R has a circumference of $2\pi R$ where $\pi = 3.14159...$ This result is not exact as π is not exact. Nevertheless, a perfectly round wheel has an exact circumference

"Of course! That is because you don't have debts," Francoise replies. "Besides that, my guarantee is *trustworthy* unless you have ill will."

Her husband raises his eyes to heaven and sighs as his only response.

Addressing him, I say, "That which is trustworthy became mysterious faith when the Middle Ages imposed dogmatic belief, at the same time that it moved away from universal norms. *Money cannot make you happy, give it to us!* Taking the reins of what they called *earthly power* became the principle motor of the spiritual hierarchy, which was losing all credibility."

"We cannot ignore the fact that science has been swept away by the wind of forgetfulness and the storm of obscurantism." Trying to convince him, I add, "The Book of the Dead of the Egyptians says that: *The principle of life was the act of doubling the principal unity in two opposite, balanced principles,* meaning the past and the future, *which engender a new life,* meaning the present."

Charles does not seem surprised and adds, "Plato also wrote in Timaeus-Critias: *Between the being indivisible and always the same,* meaning what we call the past, *and the divisible being that becomes incarnate,* meaning our future, *a mixture of the two made a third type of being,* your definition of the present."

I agree, "that idea of past, present and future, we find in the Book of Revelation: *I am the Alpha and the Omega,* says the Lord God, *He is, He was, He will come.* These are the words of Plato, five centuries before: *It is about the division of time. Of course we say that He was, He is and He will be, but to speak the truth, only the expression He is is applied to the Being that is eternal.*[2]"

---

2. Timaeus and Critias. In Greek, the time divisions are translated as Ora (,Ωρα').

"Yes, but," he continues to my great surprise, "it was the Egyptians who taught Plato the separation or doubling of the times of a sole creator: *I am yesterday and I know tomorrow...Yesterday gave birth to me, I am here Today, I create the Tomorrows...When from the other shore, I will see the other I...*[3]

He smiles slightly seeing the surprise on my face.

"Do you know where I get my information?" he asks, "from your book! And I could also add that before Plato, Pythagoras, known for his famous theorem, spoke of triad which includes the Monad of the One God, the Quaternary of the creatures and the Septenary of the doubles. So we find your seven times, which, in the doubling theory, separate the past from the future with the fourth time being the present.[4] If you think that I haven't read your book, you are mistaken! Later on, the Christians preached the Divine Trinity, the Father, the Son and the Holy Ghost, nevertheless, without situating humanity in relationship to this definition, confusing God and Son of Heaven." While speaking, he opens my book and starts reading it, exactly like his son had previously done. "Nowadays, there still exist African tribes who speak of their double. The Australian aborigines use their *image* to travel in their dreams."

After having waited for his father to finish talking, Aurelian comes into the sitting room. "They knew that *God made man in his image.* And I know why it is an image," he adds jovially. *Ana* is the doubling[5], because in Greek, the letter *a* corresponds to the number one and

---

3. The Egyptian Book of the Dead ed. Eva von Dassow, trans. Raymond Faulkner.
4. See Annex of Change your Future through the Time Openings.
5. In Greek, ana is the doubling of the a=1, with the bifurcation n (nu = ν). It is the On High, the inaccessible, the Creator; ana-b (b = 2) is the second doubling which makes the creatures; ana-g (g = 3) is the doubling of the creature or an envoy (*elos* in Greek, *el* in Hebrew) of the Creator in the future, that is ana-g-elos which means *time messenger* and not the mysterious angel with its current conotation.

the Creator is the *first*. The *n* is a bifurcation that doubles the one into two ones, without knowing why, only because you say so. The double is also *ana-g-elos*, because the *g*, which I don't know what it is, but I know that it is not an angel at all. And *man* is also an *ana* something, in Greek, which allows you to say that it is not a man like us..." I start laughing but he goes ahead. "Can you explain it to me better, I am going to try and understand."

"For what? It won't be of any use to you!"

"My father always says that ignorance is servitude and knowledge, liberty. Right, Dad?"

To our great surprise, his father bursts into laughter that becomes contagious. The child turns towards me.

"Come on! Instead of laughing senselessly, explain this *man in his image* to us. My father hasn't been able to."

"Anthropos, which in Greek means *man*, is the rough sketch of the Ana-g-elos,[6] at the end of the times. In fact the ana-g-elos of the third time, in Greek, (g=3), in the ninth time becomes, in Greek, (th=9), the Ana-th-ropos because *ropos* means draft or rubbish that is perfected at the end of each end of time."

Satisfied and obedient to his mother, Aurelian goes back to finish his homework.

---

6. See previous footnote.

26

The loss of immortality
and the return of the prodigal son

A short while later we are not surprised to see Aurelian return to the sitting room with a grumpy face.

"You are making too much noise," he grumbles, "I can't study and besides that, I have a question going round and round in my head: if something truly exists somewhere else, which allows me to be immortal, what then have we done with our immortality?"

Such a serious question, coming from the mouth of a ten-year-old child, leaves us quite perplexed.

"We are no longer immortal," I say, "because we played a terrible joke at the beginning of the cycle, 25,000 years ago."

"What joke are you talking about?" asks the young man, who is much more curious than his father.

"A mortal joke," Lucile answers. "It was Adam and Eve."[1]

"Was that mortal joke, the original sin?" asks Francoise.

---

1. See Annex of Change your Future through the Time Openings. In Greek, Adam is the doubling of α in the fourth time ($\delta = 4$) in order to obtain the best present m between the past alpha and the future omega, that is Adam. In the eighth time ($\eta = 8$) a second doubling ($\beta = 2$) produces hebe or Eve.

"Yes, it is the well-known *original sin,* but in the Greek sense of *disastrous future potential,* which we have been speaking of. This same potential that, at this moment, is bothering you with Aurelian, but which is also disturbing the entire planet." As I read scepticism in Charles' face, I specify "The future of the doubles is mortal given that they don't benefit from information exchanges with the Creator during the 25,000 years of doubling. No creature ventures there; minerals, vegetables and animals develop there without any information other than that of the doubles who are interested in that. The creature, who visits it during this cycle, modifies his future however he wishes, like a creator, but runs a great risk. We have run this risk and know first hand, that in our day, immortality does not belong to our world."

Francoise intervenes. "So tell me, what is a planet like ours good for?"

"An immortal creature only comes at the end of the doubling times, that famous end of time! He has one thousand years between two cycles,[2] however he cannot live there alone."

"Why not?" Charles asks with more interest than he shows.

"By leaving the double in the past in order to explore the dangerous future, an immortal stops having personal information from his future. How can he keep being immortal without a future that allows indispensable anticipation? No more instincts, no more intuitions, no more foresight: the only solution is to find another immortal who wants to live in the future. This accomplice substitutes the double. The joke can only be made by two: Adam and Eve were the first ones to do it. The problem quickly becomes complicated as those who were accomplices in the beginning become strangers and, at times, enemies in the end. They are, what the ancients called, demons or fallen angels who create hellish futures for us."

---

2. See Chapter 2.

"We too," Lucile carries on, "have done the same as they have; only we don't know who our Adam and our Eve are. In order to re-make our unity at the end of time, we must destroy the dangerous futures that we have created. To do this we must incarnate in the present, leaving our double in the past. This incarnation makes us take on the body of a mortal."

"How is that?"

"On Earth, it was the body of a monkey. It could have been that of a dolphin or that of any animal judged worthy of making a creature evolve. *You will give birth with pain and you will earn your bread by the sweat of your brow* says the Creator to the culprits. As we have also played the same joke, this is the only way that we have to erase the tip that we have built in the future, the enormous tip that impedes our return to the kingdom where we have been." Detecting scepticism in Charles' face, I quickly add, "it is the well-known paradise that opposes the hells of the future, there where those we now call entities or evil spirits live. And this comforts us, as we spend our time doubting their existence."

"That's what Dad does! He says that all that doesn't exist."

We don't have to wait for his father's response. "Admit it, Aurelian; it is difficult to think that the future is an imperceptible reality as real as our own."

"However we should know and modify this future before being invaded at the end of time by those that create it. There have already been dangerous invasions. They were the gods which our ancestors talked about."

Charles intervenes cuttingly with a disturbed look. "That's enough; you're going to end up convincing me."

"I wouldn't mind that," adds the child. "That way, you would see what I see and you could help me to make all the things that bother me disappear."

"You should consider," Lucile says to Charles, "that in our attempt to re-establish our union with our double, we will be the invaders of a world of light that will consider us inhabitants of their darkness. It will also be difficult for them to take us in happily. Do you know the parable of the prodigal son from the Gospels?"

"I have made sure to forget it," answers Charles, who like all savage intellectuals, knows how to hide what he doesn't know or what he doesn't want to memorise.

"Dad doesn't at all like stories that make him dream."

"The father kills the fatted calf when the prodigal son returns home!" his mother, who till now has not dared to speak up, tells him. "And his brother who has not left his father's home, always obedient to his orders, becomes jealous. But the father says to him: *Son, you are always with me and all mine is yours, but it is fitting to celebrate and be glad, because your brother who was dead, has come back to life; he was lost and has been found.*"

Charles is dumbfounded. Aurelian, satisfied, turns towards us happily. "I love it when my mother tells stories, she's brilliant! With an only child like me, my father has never killed the fatted calf, he prefers skinny cows. Diet over here, diet over there. There's not a lot to be happy about. He should try the prodigal son theme. Ah, maybe my mum's problem has to do with all that."

"What do you mean?" his mother asks nervously.

"The lack of a fatted calf at home! I was also scared to death and have come back to life because of you," he points at my wife and me, before speaking to his mother again. "Instead of celebrating a party and being glad, Dad sends me off to my room to do my homework, while you cook him something good to eat."

After this comment, Charles looks the other way, while we attend to our plate so as not to take part.

"You are right!" exclaims his mother getting up brusquely, almost furiously. Without saying anything she goes to the kitchen and comes back with a glass, a plate and silverware which she places in front of Aurelian. "You are the child who comes back home, not even the prodigal son, but the loved son who comes to celebrate with us, while your father is waiting to see if God exists in his little head."

"That is an excellent idea! Excuse me, I must make an urgent phone call. I'll be back in a few minutes."

"An urgent call at this hour?" his wife wonders.

With no further comment, he gets up, leaves his serviette on the table and with a slight smile to his son goes out of the room with a decided step, leaving us with great uncertainty as to his intentions. Aurelian breaks the silence.

"Don't worry, Mum. Otherwise you'll update a future which will prove that you were right to worry about. It'd be better to celebrate the prodigal son that I am!" he adds with a rascally face.

A few minutes later Charles comes back with a hat on his head and a clown's nose. He's holding a bottle of French champagne and a shoe box which he leaves on the table.

"The police inquiry has been fruitful. The two assailants have been arrested. According to the inspector with whom I have just spoken, Aurelian is no longer at risk. I have no fatted calf, but I do have this." He sits down and gives the box to his son. "I was thinking of giving you this tomorrow, but as God has come to give us a push tonight, here you are!"

Aurelian removes the top. A puppy raises its nose and looks at us fearfully. Too excited to speak, the child picks the dog up and holds it next to his heart, crying, he goes to embrace his father.

"You had said that we would never have a dog in the house."

"No, I have always said to you that *it would be inconceivable to have a dog in the house*! That's why I call him *Inconceivable.*"

Aurelian starts laughing, showing his unlimited happiness.

"I think," his father tells him without wanting to show his emotion, "that the only potential for this animal today is to poo all over the place, so be careful!"

27

To help others, it is necessary to have their consent

The next morning, a blue sky, sunshine and a mischievous puppy wait for us along with Aurelian and Octavia. The girl shyly turns towards me.

"Aurelian hasn't known how to tell me everything. What is it I must do or mustn't do to be sure of travelling like a rocket at night...?"

Aurelian jokingly adds, "Fasten your seatbelts, return your seat to the upright position!"

Before he finishes, I warn him, "Don't make fun of what you aren't familiar with. These days the trip is easy but the de-corporation is dangerous and the obstacles are many. Nevertheless, they are resumed in three words: will, doubt and fear."

"Thy will be done!" Aurelian exclaims. "I know, you shouldn't pray to get something, but why is doubt an obstacle?"

"Doubt is also uncertainty, perplexity, hesitation, reserve, prudence, reticence, lack of belief, suspicion, uneasiness, etc."

The young man protests "Oh no! You're not going to list each one of the synonyms from the dictionary for us. We're not in class."

"That is only to demonstrate that doubt is everywhere. It lets you suppose that you are the only one that can find the best solution to your problems, since you doubt everything, even your double whom in this way you abandon. On the other hand, your certainty as to his effectiveness makes him even more effective. Fear is also dread, anguish, apprehension, tension, terror, emotion, phobias, uneasiness, anxiety, abandon, misplacement, worry, terror..."

This enumeration bores Aurelian who sighs, "Hey! Are you going to get started again or what?"

"This is also so that you understand how hard it is for us to accept a solution which is different from our own. An ailing person wishes to be cured, a poor person, rich, a depressed person, happy, a barefooted person, heeled, a homeless person, housed, a deprived person, provided for, etc. Is this what our double recommends? At times we impose our solution because it appears to us to be the least anguishing, we don't realise that it may not be. It is, therefore, dangerous to ask our double to avoid dangerous futures."

My small conversation partner looks very worried. "I feel danger coming and I am afraid."

"If we pray in fear of tomorrow, we activate everything that makes us afraid, pushing away our double and with him all tranquillity and safety."

Octavia doesn't agree. "Nevertheless, every day thousands of millions of people who are afraid of war, come together to pray for peace!"

"And what they get is war, given that they pray in fear of it. The future will send them proof that they are right to be afraid, making them update catastrophes. Asking for and accepting with absolute trust the solution that our double offers us is the only valid prayer for obtaining a better future. Only the Muslims pray in groups without indicating an objective. That is the way they leave to Allah and his prophet the choice of what *is already written* in the future and forget that all can be erased."

"Insh Alla!" concludes Aurelian, proud of his response.

"What we must not forget is that solitude is the best shield against parasitizing. Thoughts only modify the future while words modify thoughts of those that listen to them. Teaching a truth doesn't upset anyone, praying in community modifies and can disturb everyone's potential. Jesus who was at the same time a Jew, a Palestinian and the first Christian..."

Aurelian is surprised to discover this fact. "With a passport like that, he'd have a hard time getting by these days."

"Jesus taught in the synagogues and then went into the wild alone to pray. Curiously, contrary to his example, Christians unite to pray in churches, often to ask for their wishes to come true or asking for help for those who have not asked them for anything."

Octavia, surprised, opens her eyes very wide. "So I can't help Aurelian if he doesn't ask me to?"

"You mustn't ever use your dreams to help someone without having asked his permission beforehand."

"Why not?"

"Because you can modify his future and without Aurelian's acceptance, you become responsible for its modifications and of its consequences."

"If the future that she creates," comments Aurelian, "is better than mine, is she then responsible for the improvement?"

"How do you know if it is better? Only your double knows that."

"But Octavia knows that I agree with her helping me to be all right."

"For you to be well, your thoughts must change. If they change because of Octavia and not because of you, your problem will still be there and besides that, it could get worse. In that case, you must know that your change is due to Octavia and not to you. If not, once you've been cured, you will feel the temptation to impose your ideas on the pretext that they have brought about a solution.

This is how you can promote lies that the future needs, so as to live like it wants."

"Well, all right. But I have to be able to help those that need help!"

"In order to help someone, I have already told you, it is enough to think of doing to others as you would like them to think of doing to you. This is the only rule which frees you from all the evils of the future and does not implicate your responsibility in future disorders. This liberation will allow you to be able to reunite with your double at the end of time. Formerly, it was said that in this way the creating parcel within you didn't die. In ancient Greece, the death of an immortal was said *moros* and the absence of death *amoros*, that means the true divine *love* that desires, and therefore creates in the future, the immortality of all his creatures. It is not about the love that everyone talks about. Love each other as ourselves is an energetic law that hands us the key to immortality. And Yeshua, the Aramean, who gave us this vital universal law, is, because of that, the greatest of all the wise men."

Aurelian opens his eyes extremely wide. "According to you, is love a physical law?"

"Careful! *Amoros* is a law and love is a feeling. I can hate a hateful person and have thoughts of *amoros,* which from here on I will call benevolence, towards them. For example, I do not like a killer, however I can think, or not think, of doing to him what I would like him to think, or not think, of doing to me. That is how I can avoid the idea of vengeance. *Amoros* (benevolence) is not love, but it leads to it by doing away with all hateful thoughts and so brings about compassion. It allows the exchange of the best potentials. It is the rule for universal survival. You must obey it if you don't want your double to disintegrate and you, along with him, to become lost energies. Hate and the thoughts that hate engenders lead to a destructive future potential that can bring about the death (moros) of your double."

Francoise, who up to now had kept silent, intervenes. "Then, why not help all those who are ignorant of this?"

"Because they are not asking for anything! If our thoughts create interesting futures in benevolence, then those that make use of it will live well. It is enough for them to also be in benevolence to also have access to them. This is the one and only valid rule which grants freedom to everybody!"

"And if the person I want to help is in coma, what can I do? Give up on helping them?"

"Of course not, nevertheless, as soon as the person comes out of coma, it is necessary to tell them of the help that you have provided without their consent."

"Who wouldn't want to be helped?"

A surprising story comes to mind. "A man was in hospital dying of a ravaging leukaemia. He was on artificial respiration. The doctors had given him no hope for survival. A friend we have in common came to ask for our assistance. She was greatly surprised when three days later this gravely ill man's health improved. When, upon our urging, our friend commented to this man the how and the why of his recuperation, do you know what he said?"

"Thank you so much!"

"Not at all! He was furious and said: *Who is the bastard that has done this to me?* It must be said that he had just lost his son to AIDS and that he wanted to be reunited with him. His healing was not at all welcome. After having been completely healed, he died a year later after a heart attack, without resistance, I was going to say *cured.* Helping someone without having asked their permission is very dangerous because you take charge of the potentials of the person that you are helping."

"Before you were saying that a mother can ask for help for her own mother or for her children, right?"

"Exactly, providing that she knows what she is doing. So many mothers make their children ill or schizophrenic without knowing it, only because of the information from the future that they don't know how to control!"

"Why is the information from the future always dangerous?"

"It's the consequence of our lies, criticism and false accusations and permanent judgements that we update without reflection. Our unfitting thoughts create, in the future, what the good grounds of our envies show us. We must therefore distrust intuitions that can come to us from our future. They are not safe and come with the appearance of truth. On the other hand, our double has no reason to lie to or mislead us given that we would immediately create a dangerous or useless future potential for him."

"Yes, but," Octavia warns, "if he doesn't have the adequate information about us..."

Aurelian cuts her off. "If he is misinformed, it is because you have not given him good information!"

I interrupt thim. "It can also be that you are unaware of your true problems. In any case, if he doesn't know you well, because you don't know him well, he will give you incomprehensible information and will arrange your future without taking into account your life. You could suffer the consequences."

"But then, what is it that we have to do?" they say in unison.

"Guide him through your thankfulness. If we thank him, he will know that he is on the right path and not doubt about going ahead with what he has begun. To do this we must know ourselves well and not give thanks for something that we think is good. On the other hand, giving thanks ahead of time, for whatever it may be, is dangerous. This could update a painful potential, difficult to bare. If, besides this, you consider physical or psychic pain as a gift from God, you will make the situation worse."

"Why?"

"Our double's objective is not at all to make us suffer; he desires to create a pleasant potential. For him, as well as us, suffering doesn't lead to anything good and cannot in any case be put upon a pedestal. Suffering in order to live better is a stupidity instilled by the future, never by our doubles."

"Difficult, difficult," sighs Octavia, "you knock a lot of things off balance."

"There is a good point of reference. Balance is solid when it allows you to build a future without danger to others. The change in our thoughts is more important than the restoration of our body."

"You see," says Aurelian to Octavia, "I told you so, it's the thoughts. It's amazing."

"It is often difficult to change as lies are well-rooted within us, due to an excessive parasitizing of the future during our dreams."

"If dreams are lies," says Octavia, "maybe Aurelian is not my boyfriend, because I dream of being with him. With your stories, I have the feeling of being closed up in the future and I'm losing my courage."

Aurelian is dumbstruck. His mother and I laugh merrily, which he doesn't at all like.

"That's not funny! She's right, you know. So many older people make mistakes then later get separated. Why couldn't this happen with us? And besides that, we're not even married yet!"

About to burst into tears, he leaves the room slamming the door on his way out.

Octavia gets up. "I am going to tell him what he has explained to me and forgotten," she says with her little voice and very serious aspect.

"What is it that he has forgotten?" asks Aurelian's mother.

"He said that if I get furious, I create a bigger rage in the future to prove to myself that my previous anger was justified. If, later on, I'm very furious, I create an enormous fury in the future to prove that my big rage was even more justified than the small one. So, I'm going to talk to him before he creates a rage as big as himself, because I know that he is my boyfriend forever!"

We await her exit in silence, before hiding our emotion with a laugh, through which our infinite tenderness can be glimpsed.

28

The Twelve Doors of the Zodiac

Octavia has hardly left when Charles bursts back in. After a quick greeting, he comments to his wife an event whose unsettling aspect he cannot hide.

"They want Aurelian to come down to identify his aggressors."

"But, why?" Francoise asks.

"Those *pigs* deny everything." I feel that Charles is full of doubt. "Aurelian can't see them; it'll cause him to have a relapse. It was too good to be true!"

"Don't ever think like that!" Lucile protests. "Otherwise the future will prove you right in thinking that it is too good to be true. You have to erase that thought!"

"You don't know how sensitive Aurelian is!"

"Yes, we saw him when he was playing the violin. Anyway, he mustn't harvest a fear that doesn't belong to him under the pretext that you are afraid he'll be frightened."

"I have to see the inspector this afternoon," Charles adds, not very convinced. "Tomorrow at mid-day we'll see if Aurelian can stand the shock and if, due to this, the solar explosions calm down, the ice at the poles doesn't melt, the Earth's axis doesn't waver. Let's see..." he interrupts his speech and sighs deeply at the same time he throws me a mocking look."

We say good-bye to everyone, wishing them a good night.

The next day a call from Charles gladdens our hearts.

"I have put a bottle of French Champagne in the fridge, could you come over for an aperitif? I have very good news and I would like to beg your pardon for...let's say, for my pessimism."

A short while later we drink to Aurelian's health, who has identified his aggressors without showing the least fear. He has gotten over his troubles, his mother is radiant and his father is intoning a "*mea culpa.*"

While the ladies go off to the kitchen, Charles makes use of the time that we are together to finally expulse the superior intellectual that sleeps within him. "Yesterday you told me that I must erase my pessimistic thoughts. How can I do that? I wouldn't want to be, through ignorance, the cause of a relapse for Aurelian."

"Don't worry, not all the futures are available at the same time. Aurelian still has resources. The potentials are warehoused in twelve different spaces. The movement of the planets in our solar system is what regulates the openings of the twelve doors. You have probably read in our book that anticipatory information comes from the twelve planetary spaces that two by two separate the seven doubling times."[1] Seeing Charles' undecided air, I add, "Remember the Greeks said that each one of those spaces was a servant of life, or a zoi-diakonos or zodiac."

"How can a space be at my service?"

"There exist times of opening and closing that our ancestors well knew and studied from the planetary movements."

"Are you talking about the astrological or zodiacal tables?"

"Yes, of course. As they already knew that with the passing of millenniums, we would believe ourselves to be wise monkeys climbing

---

1. See Annex of Change your Future through the Time Openings.

in the trees," I say jokingly, "they left us a simple teaching with the twelve constellations that are shown on the horizon of our earthly orbit: Aries, Taurus, Gemini, Cancer, Leo, etc... We understand the mechanism of these antique tables that were established according to a rigorous scientific law. They allowed us to find the most favourable moments for what we wished to undertake, in relation to the available potentials."

"Haven't you said before that this understanding is no longer valid since March 1989, since all the doors are now open?"

"All the valid information is continually at our disposal."

"Which means that astrology is useless these days?"

"No, on the contrary. Well understood, it would allow us to know our weaknesses as well as our virtues according to the time of our conception and the time of our birth. If we knew how to keep in mind our zodiacal origins, we would become much more efficient and our association with other people would be more sensible. But who knows these dates accurately? Formerly, children were conceived at a concrete time, chosen by wizards and, in addition to that, all births were natural."

"You know that nowadays, a child is rarely born on the weekend. Doctors and mid-wives are on holiday and try to modify the birth date. How can we take the time of birth as truly valid for your astrology? Who, these days, would use the astrological tables before the act of procreation?"

"Why not give it a try? Do you think that a double is not capable of sending intuition to parents, mid-wives and the baby herself?"

"That would be logical. I agree with you."

29

Three Days of Balance, Forty Days of Stabilization

Almost scandalised, Charles exclaims, "You're not going to tell me that you believe in the horoscope? But there is nothing scientific about it!"

"In Greek" I tell him, "*Ora* meant the division of time and *scopos*, white. The horoscope was the *ascendant*, the emanation of *Man* towards the son of man. It had to be consulted each day as the tables indicated the rules which must be respected in order to receive information from the past and the future."

"Isn't this reception automatic?"

"No, it depends upon how long the time openings last, which must always be imperceptible for us, so as to give us the sensation that they do not exist. In the slowed-down time of our double, each one of them lasts no longer than three days of our time. Nevertheless, each one of ours corresponds to forty days in the future. This universal law is fundamental."

"Is there any relationship between these forty days and the forty days of Lent?" asks Charles intrigued.

"Yes, of course. One of our thoughts immediately creates forty days of potential in the future. Fortunately, that future cannot be immediately used."

"Why do you say *fortunately*? Wouldn't it be better to always have everything immediately?"

"A thought creates a future that you cannot update immediately."

"If I ask myself a question, the future finds the answer in less time than it takes me to formulate it. Isn't that what you have been telling us?"

"Yes, but it is not immediately available. In the meantime, you must find another in an already existing potential. That's why the solution is often not adequate for your problem. So you reject it and forget the thought that, having been released, always bares fruit. Good or bad, green, ripe or rotten, they will be picked later on by you or by whomever has a similar thought."

"How can it be that time elapses between the question and the answer?"

"It's protection. If it were possible to create and immediately update a future, our responsibility would be dreadful."

"Why?"

"Through our thoughts, we create dangers without realising it. For example, you attack a person who jostles you in the street. His cheekiness makes you feel like killing him. Instantaneously, a future killer is created in your time openings."

"What does it matter if I don't kill anyone?"

"You can be responsible for a misfortune. Imagine that a stranger charges at a pedestrian who shoves him and whose ill will makes him feel like murdering him. This story, similar to yours, gives him immediate access to the future that you have created. New ideas, which without you he wouldn't have had, come to his mind. If this man kills the pedestrian, who is responsible?"

Aurelian's father finally realises the power of a forgotten thought and his face contracts even more. "Your idea is completely hellish!"

"And demoniacal, if you dare say so! The Hell of the future is full of bad and often dangerous intentions. On the television, a journalist reports how this murder has taken place, this barbarity turns your stomach, but it would never occur to you to think that you are also responsible for this and that by judging the criminal, you are judging yourself."

"If nobody thought about killing, could nobody then kill?"

"It is not that simple. If nobody had thought about killing for the last 25,000 years, no killing potential would exist on Earth and murder would be impossible. Unfortunately, after Adam and Eve's offence, along came Cain, whose name let us not forget means to kill in Greek.[1] In fact this couple was the first in directing our potential towards madness: murder was made reality among creatures that had never before thought of it."

Suddenly Charles becomes conscious of the great responsibility he has towards his son. Bewilderment is read in his eyes, his tone of voice becomes serious. "You realise that you are scaring me with your story of responsibilities! Perhaps Aurelian has suffered due to my thoughts. First I thought he was lying, then I criticised him. So, I have created, in my future, material to prove to myself that my lies and my criticism were correct."

"Exactly! A father, who thinks *whatever* about his son, constructs that *whatever* for him."

"What do you do so that this *whatever* is not useable?"

"Thank goodness that you have forty days to erase it. Your double and your dreams are there for that. That is the way that, by calming the future each night through your dreams, you stabilise the entire planet, because the law is very simple: if nobody thought about killing for forty days and if our doubles erased this possibility from our future, murder on Earth would be impossible."

---

1. See Annex of Change your Future through the Time Openings.

"Now I understand the importance of Lent. You say that, long before Christianity, in all the Celtic villages, three clairvoyants chosen at random had to resolve the problems that affected the people."

"They ordered the greatest madness till Shrove Tuesday which was happily celebrated around a large bonfire. Afterwards, on Wednesday, closing the eyes of clairvoyance with ashes, they began the forty days of Lent in order to let their doubles select the new futures and erase the bad ones. On the fortieth day, the village came back to life with the first *branches* of spring. Intuitions and signs multiplied, their problems were resolved. Forty days to find the best solution, three days to live it. All of our intuitions are based on this cycle."

"Nevertheless, many times they are not at all interesting."

"Because they are the consequence of not very interesting, completely forgotten past projects. Nevertheless, once the project has been examined, the future always looks for multiple ways to resolve it. On the fortieth day, the solution, either placebo or nocebo, can be updated by whoever considers this same problem."

My conversation partner changes his opinion. "The resurrection of Jesus on the third day, does it have something to do with your three days?"

30

On the Frontier of Death: Near Death Experience and Resurrection

"Resurrection is a universal law."

Francoise and Lucile come back in this moment. Relieved and happy by the arrival of the women, Charles exclaims "Thank goodness, you've finally come back!" and addressing my wife, adds "if not, your husband would have demonstrated to me that resurrection is a well-established physical law and the worst part is that I would have ended up believing it, as he can be very convincing."

Lucile agrees. "He would have been right, as resurrection is a universal law known by ancient civilisations."

Charles nods, but with some reservations. "In fact, I have read your book and I have confirmed all of it in the old manuscripts. It is also true that resurrection on the third day appears in the tablets of the Sumerians: the goddess Inanna come back from a stay amongst the dead after that amount of time, thanks to her vizier Ninshubur. It is also written that she crossed seven doorways."

"Me too," exclaims Aurelian while smiling at Octavia, "I resuscitated on the third day. When I woke up in the morning I was no longer afraid of anything. Nevertheless, I had only opened two doors, the door to my room and the door to the bathroom to look at myself in the mirror." Seeing Octavia's expression and feeling uncomfortable, he adds "I know that those doors don't have anything to do with the other ones. Who do you take me for anyway?"

"For my vizier, that's all!" says Octavia teasingly. "Am I not your adored goddess?"

Francoise intervenes and asks them to listen.

"Those three days are very important. In our world, the double can make use of this time to send us back to Earth after our death. In order to assure a person's decease, it is always necessary to wait three days. Like Jesus, but for very different reasons, we can resuscitate on the third day. Let me explain: detected by the absolute inactivity of our brain, clinical death is only a dream that takes us towards the light of our double. At first, we pass through a dark tunnel where we discover all our future potentials. After three days, death becomes irresistible. The water of our body loses its information. Our ancestors knew this and never interred the dead before this period of time. Nowadays, no on pays attention to this, however gravediggers have confirmed that thirty per cent of the cadavers disinterred have moved in their graves. The water was re-informed by their double."

"My mother told me," screams Octavia, excited by a story that has just come to mind, "that her father sat up in his coffin, in the same moment that they were going to close the lid, and begged everyone's pardon. My grandmother had a heart attack and they were buried together, because my grandfather died again even before knowing that he had resuscitated, but he left a message for each one of his children."

Aurelian, sceptical, starts laughing. "Have you seen that on the telly?"

"No, it's true!" protests Octavia. "Ask my mum about it!"

I intervene in order to defend the young lady. "What we're talking about are Near Death Experiences or NDE. These occurrences have been being studied since a long time ago, they are frequent and always reveal similar characteristics. It has even been possible to establish a specific scientific protocol based on millions of testimonies."

"What is that protocol?" asks Charles, always so passionate about the objections that he is able to make.

"A person in a NDE hears the people around them, who sometimes talk about their death as an irreversible reality. They are not able to communicate and after the sound of a pop, leave their body and at times assist from outside of themselves with the emergency measures or reanimation of their body. Afterwards they are aspirated through a dark tunnel where they discover other people, often deceased people close to them, before arriving in front of a being of light. Solicitous, this luminous being gives them good advice that this person often memorises and becomes aware of an un-crossable frontier, before the shadow aspirates them violently. It is then when the deferred dead person finds themselves alive and normally this unexpected return brings about a radical change in their behaviour."

"Our paradoxical sleep" adds Lucile, "is similar to this curious experience of imminent death. The difference stems from the fact that an energetic body comes immediately into us to assure our survival during the information exchanges. During NDE, our organism is abandoned and can start to decompose. Only our return after three days can put it back on its feet."

Nothing escapes Aurelian's attention, who intervenes at once. "I would like to know if three days are enough to be able to say that I will never again be afraid of anything."

Seeing the extremely sad faces of Octavia and Francoise, I specify, "We always need those famous forty days to be able to make use of the twelve planetary doors and obtain the best solution to our problem of the first day. Not everything can always be arranged in one dream. The planets don't speed up their course in order to please us. Our double can open only one of the twelve zodiacal doors during three days."

Lucile turns towards Aurelian. "Don't worry! It is behind that first door that yours has found a future capable of making you better and has expulsed the one that made you suffer."

"So," adds the young man addressing his mother with a happy smile, "being patient is enough. To open the twelve doors takes thirty-six days. It isn't difficult, I've already found out!"

"It also takes an information synthesis, which is carried out in three days. Altogether it makes up a cycle of thirty-nine days."

"Can't it go any faster?" asks Octavia.

"Yes, but we would need to have twelve doubles in addition to our own, like Jesus and his twelve apostles. The information would be instantaneously selected by the twelve and the thirteenth would make the synthesis."

"Jesus prayed alone in the desert and needed forty days to find a solution to his problem."

"The solution and the temptation of a future potential. In fact the Prince of Darkness came to tempt him with his solutions, which already existed in the dark kingdom. The fortieth day is always the first day of a new cycle. The forty days of Lent and quarantine are the necessary cleansing of the spirit and the body. If we continue forward with the daily information exchanges with our double, six successive cycles allow the analysis and arranging of the six double spaces of the zodiac before making a synthesis during the seventh."

"Seven cycles of forty days are necessary in a pregnancy. The last forty days are used to make the synthesis. Interrupting this cycle can be dangerous. That is why a premature infant of six times forty days can live without any problem. Nevertheless a baby, who is born prematurely during the seventh and last period, is much more fragile. Obstetricians have become aware of this *curious* fragility, but have never been able to explain the reason for it. However it seems evident that a good analysis is more valuable than an interrupted synthesis."

"In reality, a child and his double make use of an imperceptible time to become aware of the future of the parents during their sexual act. Fertilisation is only possible if the implied potential is convenient for them. On the third day, the foetus disposes of a future of forty days. Life does not exist within the ovum before that time, only a preparation for terrestrial life, a sort of resurrection of the future in the present."

While I am explaining all of this, the answer that Francoise has been waiting for can be seen on her face. "So taking the morning-after pill would not be an abortion!"

Seeing her great surprise, I specify "That is even more correct when we find out that the water, necessary for life to warehouse information, only comes into the ovum on the sixth day."

"We can then say that a child makes use of forty days in the future before the seven times forty days in the present. Besides that, we must add the forty days after birth that allows the double to have a first potential in our present. After giving birth, the mother feels a great difference; she misses the suggestions of the double, a great emptiness is created within her as all of a sudden her body longs for the vital information. This is the situation that sometimes develops into a *postpartum depression*."

"How can that be avoided?"

"A sole exchange with the double can re-establish an entire family, in three days, with a new potential of forty days. Look at the resurrection of Jesus! He had this time on Earth available to him after his death. The fortieth day could bring him near a future potential created on the first day. Its updating would have brought about a new responsibility in the future. His departure was therefore necessary to avoid this dangerous link."

31

Jesus

Charles' scepticism is no longer felt, just the opposite! His question multiply, each one wrapped up in an evident curiosity.

"In what moment do you situate Jesus in your time cycle?"

"The solar doubling cycle is divided into twelve periods: the six days and six nights of the Bible. Each 2070 years, an immortal creature comes to help us. Also called *avatar*, the last of the twelve was Yeshua, the Aramean. Like all immortals, he is found in the past of his double and in the future of the Creator and so can say *I am in the father and the father is in me.*"

Charles nods his head, showing that he no longer opposes with his habitual intellectual reticence.

"This arrival was prepared for by an entire nation during the last biblical day. *It was necessary!* Recall the two prophets that took charge of the opening and closing of the doors between the world of the mortals and that of the immortals, also called Jerusalem Celeste. I am speaking about Buddha who was born some 630 years before Christ and of Mohammed who died in the year 632 after Christ. It is not a coincidence: the opening brought Buddha closer to his double and the closing moved away Mohammed from his. This double consequence was evident. In fact, Buddha's youth was intransigent, at times violent, Mohammed's was tolerant and pacific. Their old age was the opposite: Buddha was tolerant and pacific while Mohammed was intransigent and at times violent. Regarding Jesus, he was able to benefit from a perfect balance."[1]

"Curiously," points out Francoise, "Buddhism, Christianity and Islam direct the current three great spiritual movements. Instead of confronting each other, they should be complementing each other!"

I completely agree. "And they did. The message of Buddha, Jesus and Mohammed was simple *Do not think of doing to others what you do not want them to think of doing to you!* What Jesus also summed up by saying: *Love one another as yourselves!* He could have explained doubling, but in that epoch, *no one had eyes to see with, nor ears to hear."*

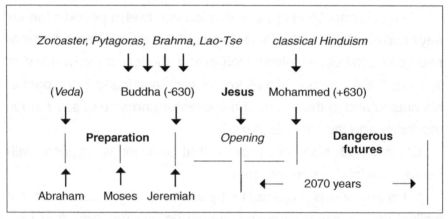

The Time Opening (two times 630 years)

---

1. This transition lasted 1080 years: imagine a river of time with six locks for changing levels. Six locks to enter our time and six locks to leave it, with each gate requiring 90 years: 30 years to enter, 30 years to reach level and 30 years to leave. The twelve gates of the six locks need 630 years. Once the level has been reached, in 30 years, the first gate of the first lock of the six locks leading the way out begins to open. That only leaves 30 years of tranquillity among the twelve locks and the need to again leave in the same moment of the opening of the first gate of the first lock of the six that lead the way out.

Another explanation from Greek mythology: twelve bolts, cleis in Greek, open onto the fertile plain, hera. Twelve labours of Hera-cleis (Hercules), are necessary to obtain the twelve zodiacs specific information in order to obtain immortality.

"His death made the exploration of our future possible. It was the descent into the hellish futures, Hell, as the Greeks said, that had important consequences. In the first place, it was the return of our doubles to the future of the Creator, as they had been lost in the darkness. Then, Jesus offered them redemption. Without that our incarnation would have become impossible during the sixth and last night of the two thousand years."

Francoise is doubtful and later changes her opinion. "Isn't redemption the remission of sins of the whole of humanity?" she exclaims.

"Like many people, you are confusing two consequences. The exploration of the future by this immortal erased dangerous potentials, which means the *sins of the world* in the Greek sense of the word. That is the second consequence of his death that had to come at a concrete time: in the moment in which the doors of the future would be wide open, like right now. It was necessary to eliminate the dangerous potentials before this last biblical night of two thousand years. If not, the Prince of Darkness would have shredded us up without difficulty, making us update hellish futures. Jesus knew that this Prince had no power over him. He was the master of the future, given that he was the master of our past."

"Mustn't he come back at the end of time?"

"This end is the end of doubling. If he comes back, it will be in a non-doubled body, which the ancients called the glorious body. It is this *materialised* body that Jesus showed to his amazed apostles for forty days. This is the way he demonstrated to them his true immortal nature. Nevertheless, he must have been very worried."

"Why?" asks Aurelian who no longer appeared interested in our conversation.

"Humanity must hang on till the end of times as there are terrifiying troublemakers in the future. That is why Jesus has sent us his double, the one that is next to, *para* in Greek, the bolt *cleis*. He is the Paraclete (*para-cleis*).[2]

"No theologian talks about all that!" adds Francoise surprised.

"No theologian talks about doubling either! Nevertheless the Gospel of Saint Thomas seems to show that this essential notion was perfectly known in antiquity. *In the day when you were together, you separated,* says this Gospel[3], *moreover when you are separated, what will you do?* There is no doubt about the authenticity of this text, as it was found in Upper Egypt in the 1940's and has not had time to suffer translation errors."

"So?" Aurelian is nervous. "What are we going to do now that we continue being two?"

"Listen to the Paraclete. *What is mine shall be given you,* specifies Jesus leading us to understand that a sole thought of the double is healthy energy, vital information."

"And how do you hear it?"

"By letting your double tell you what the Paraclete says to him. Since March 1989, the *bolts* are open and He hears them live and direct."

"We no longer need intermediaries," Lucile specifies.

"But be careful! The future also hears you very well and for the moment our thoughts attract extremely dangerous potentials. Danger is at our door, desolation as well. Jesus also warned us of this: *There will be signs in the heavens, the moon and the stars.*"[4]

"What are these signs?" asks the young man.

"I have already told you: the sign of Jonah which corresponds to the arrival of new planets that are finally visible beyond Pluto. Meteorites could change their orbit brusquely."

---

2. The Gospel According to Saint John, XV 16.
3. The Gospel According to Saint Thomas XI & XXII. Apocryphal Gospel. http://en.wikipedia.org/wiki/Gospel_of_Thomas.
4. The Gospel According to Saint Luke, XXI 25.

32

The king and his subjects

This entire conversation has left Aurelian perplexed. He has understood many things, but one continues to surprise him.

"Why are you talking about all this with a kid like me? Shouldn't you be talking to famous personalities and important people? If they did what you say, everyone else would follow them and our problems would be over."

"I am going to tell you a story, so that you understand that it is better to address the young people of this world before addressing the adults. Pay attention! You too, Octavia!"

"Once upon a time there was a king who created negative potentials in order to govern his country. He never smiled at all and his future didn't either. His potential was heavy and dangerous.

His subjects lived peacefully in their dwellings, awaiting better days, never thinking of anything bad. They constructed marvellous potentials.

The king could extract from this future and live pleasant days, without knowing that he owed it to the pleasant thoughts of his subjects who lived peacefully in their dwellings, awaiting better days, never thinking of anything bad.

The king lived so stupendously well that he used himself as an example, explaining that to have it all in life, you had to know how to fight like him, squash the weak and the incapable, thanks to the potentials that he knew how to produce through his wants and desires to be a powerful king.

He lived so well that his subjects ended up asking themselves questions. Was it really worth it to live well in their dwellings, awaiting better days, never thinking anything bad, constructing marvellous potentials that probably weren't enough?

Wouldn't it be better to learn how to fight like their king, squash the weak and the incapable? This horrible temptation quickly led the king's subjects to update real, existing potentials. It did not take long to see the effects. The kingdom was driven mad by war and unprecedented catastrophes.

The king incriminated..."

"What does incriminate mean?" Octavia interrupts me.

"Incriminate is to blame," I tell her before going on with my story.

"So then, the king blamed the way of living of his subjects who lived too peacefully in their dwellings, never thinking anything bad, constructing insufficient potentials. Then, too oppressed to await better days, the subjects finally decided to think like the king. Little by little, there was no longer anything good or sweet in their potential. Everyone lived over-excited...and was unfortunate!

The moral of the story is: at the end of times, the kings will so corrupted, that corruption will reign in every country. That is the conclusion of the Book of Revelation of Saint John."

"We are extremely lucky!" Aurelian informs us.

"Why?" asks Octavia.

"In our country there is no longer a king, only a president!" he answers completely satisfied.

"Anyway, let's not throw stones at the ones that govern us. They are made in our image, as it is our thoughts that attract extremely dangerous potentials. "

33

The signs of the end and the possible benefits

Aurelian seems both amused and astonished. "Do you really think large rocks will fall from the sky?"

"Why always think of catastrophes that can be avoided? If we modify our thoughts, that grandiose spectacle will be annulled.[1] Prophets of misfortune should make amends to those who, because of them, have already reserved their place in the front row of global catastrophes."

"Nevertheless", says Françoise, "everyone says that the planet is not okay, that things are warming up and the sea level is rising."

"The level of our foolishness is too! The political world makes us believe that industrial pollution is modifying the planet. Don't be fooled, it is miniscule in comparison with the pollution of the future that our thoughts have created. The Earth, like us, updates available futures. And these are not very good because our thoughts are not either. Let's change them and the planet will recover the balance that we all need!"

---

1. See Annex of Change your Future through the Time Openings.

Aurelian opens his eyes wide. "Thoughts cannot stop a rock that is falling from the sky! That's mad!"

"The rock arrives because the Earth needs energy and it needs energy because our thoughts, which are also energy capable of creating the future, are too poor. We must enrich them!" The Earth is like us: when it doesn't receive enough energy, everything that passes by looks attractive. Nowadays, our planet is weakened by a 25,000 year fast. It could become bulimic; the doors of the future are wide open. Meteorites are its favourite food. In 2002, it attracted two enormous boulders that brushed past without us having even been able to foresee them. If they had crashed into the Earth, it would have meant the extinction of humanity, like in the time of the dinosaurs. If the Earth ingests too many rocks, it vomits them into space and so wakes up its volcanoes. It shakes it scales, which scientists call plate tectonics. Everyone should know that our detestable thoughts whet its appetite and accelerate the end of times. If I always think of doing to others what I would want them to think of doing to me, the Earth will do the same and we will harvest the benefits that it offers us at the end of times."

Always attentive, Aurelian's father intervenes. "Can the date of this end be foreseen?"

"Calculations only give us the theoretical date of 2079, but we will probably never arrive there."

"Why not?"

"The end of time arrives after six periods of thirty years.[2] The seven openings set off enormous solar explosions. For our ancestors,

2. See Chapter III: 30 years separate 1899, 1929, 1959 and 1989. Now, the doors of the past are the ones that are opening into our world. We are no longer the masters of that time. 30 years are now nothing more than theoretical periods. In 2003, a solar explosion opened the fifth period.

it was the opening of the seven seals of the Apocalypse. The first three have opened the doors of the future. For the three doors of the past all depends upon our doubles and they themselves depend upon the Creator. *As to the time,* said Jesus, *only the Father knows.*"

"Could you be a little more precise?"

"The solar explosion of 2003 shows us that the fifth seal had been opened sixteen years before the date of its theoretical opening. Due to the hurry to balance our world that creates their potentials, our doubles open the doors of our past too quickly. This acceleration is so strong that it is possible to deduce that, without a change in our behaviour, the date of the end of the seven times could coincide with the end of the Mayan calendar in December 2012. Nevertheless, now you know that no prediction, Mayan or otherwise, is definitive. It is, therefore, still possible to put this date off a few years to allow the Earth to calm down. Anyway, it can't go beyond 2079 less sixteen years, or 2063."

I would like to tell Charles that the creatures who have created our future, whom we call spirits, entities, devils, demons or extraterrestrials, have already finished their doubling. They will soon be on Earth with incredible powers, where they will pass themselves off as gods, managing dangerous futures that they will have studied and explored well before us, provoking diseases to afterwards cure them, disturbing the planet to afterwards be able to calm it. However, I know, like most so-called civilised, reasonable human beings, that it is difficult to imagine such a reality behind these intentions. And I understand it, as our parasitizing is such that our misinformation is almost absolute. Nevertheless, for a time, we are still in charge of our future. No one impedes us from re-taking our place as conductor of our orchestra and *sending our musicians back to their music stands*. It is enough for us to read the musical score that our double composes for us every night and not all the other writings, often esoteric, always sectarian, so-called inspired by God, the angels or extraterrestrials.

Books, shows, television and cinema instil concepts and cause grave errors of interpretation to the most gullible. These measures prepare for, without us being aware of it, the arrival of an exceptional being, endowed with such strength, whom we will wrongly consider a saviour of humanity, a god...so as to more easily infiltrate our fragile brains, parasitic thoughts make use of religious speech in which God and Love always have the foremost place. Because of this infernal parasitizing, unfortunately our aggressiveness currently develops as quickly as our diseases and our catastrophes.

"Do you think," Charles asks me, "that our world has already known similar periods?"

The scars of successive chaos are etched everywhere. Our scientists continually discover them in the sediments, the ice, the upheavals of the flora and fauna. Archaeological excavations are constantly surprising us. We instinctively look for the past that has unleashed such bad futures. Four thousand years before Christ, an opening to the future let in false gods: it was the time of the Sumerians and humans would discover beings who came from *other places*. After a thousand years of feats, they disappeared and left us a testament of written messages engraved upon numerous monuments and tombs."

"It is true," emphasises Charles, "that humanity was then brusquely coming out of the stone age to enter into amazing knowledge of mathematics, architecture, astronomy, agronomy, irrigation, etc."

"That is how the following generations made use of the remains of a lost knowledge: the Egypt of the Pharaohs was already unfamiliar with the universal laws and had strayed from their objective." Observing Charles' grimace of doubt. I immediately add, "Did you know that the Sphinx is, in reality, previous to the time of the Pharaohs? The erosion that it has suffered is the consequence of a rainy climate: that is how the date of its construction is deduced to be around 10,500 years before our era. This leads us to believe that the chaos of that epoch annihilated an important civilisation where great traditions originated."

"Are you talking about the Atlanteans and of the disappearance of Atlantis?" asks Francoise, whose question makes Charles smile.

"What we definitely know is that our planet was dragged towards destructive chaos and that Plato still had them in his memory: *when the divine portion began to fade away, and became diluted too often and too much with the mortal admixture, and the human nature got the upper hand,...Zeus...collected all the gods into their most holy habitation, which being placed in the centre of the world, beholds all created things. And when he had called them together, he spake as follows...*We will never know what Plato wanted Critias to say as the text ends there[3]. To call all the gods to where the futures are created, the situation must have been critical. Proof is that 97% of the superior mammals had disappeared from the Northern Hemisphere."

"Do you mean to keep terrorising us?" the always attentive Aurelian is newly nervous.

"A deluge had already once surprised and destroyed humanity who had forgotten the essential. In our time, it is still possible to calm the planet if we understand our complete responsibility in its disorder."

Charles frowns. "Are you also one of the ones who think that a great chaos is imminent, that a hellish future should punish the world?"

"The one who thinks of chaos, instantly gives birth to a chaotic hell in the future, which straight away tries to give it back to us. Clairvoyants or channellers who, being more or less inspired, predict peace on Earth while brandishing the spectre of an atrocious cataclysm, are often the very source of the same planetary chaos that they are

---

3. Timaeus and Critias by Plato.

trying to avoid. But soon the times will balance out; the sixth seal will open, spilling out a wave of very real beings who enjoy creating the future which we currently desire. How can we think that this invasion might bring peace on Earth if our projects don't become pacific?"

"Do you think that that will be enough?"

"Hate is an energy that attracts more hate and which controls the world. Why not use love which is an equally strong energy? I am not talking about the love which is spoken of by those who don't live it, but about the love that obligates us to watch out for each one of our thoughts. Without sharing the knowledge related with this love, our survival will become impossible in the coming years. The Age of Aquarius, which closes the doubling of times, blows a breath of immortality over our heads, so that we are able to re-make our unity. Before it can be like that, we will suffer very real invasions of very surprising beings."

"Are you serious?" Charles does not mind accepting the existence of other creatures in the universe as long as they stay in distant galaxies.

"Why put on a blindfold? After the sixth seal, the future must appear in its reality. This was already the case in the times of the Sumer"

To accentuate my idea, I show them the sketches from the annex of our book.

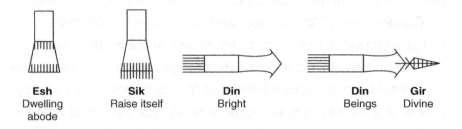

Esh	**Sik**	**Din**	**Din**	**Gir**
Dwelling abode	Raise itself	Bright	Beings	Divine

Without speaking of the Atlanteans, there have already been invaders like the fabulous heroes of the Greek Olympus, so very ungodly, or those gods of the Sumer. In the Bible, *the Nephilim were on the Earth in that time...they were strong ones of eternity, the nation of the shem...These sons of Gods coupled with daughters of men, the glorious men of that time.*[4] Nephelos, in Greek, means small clouds in the sky. In the language of the Sumer, they were identified flying objects.

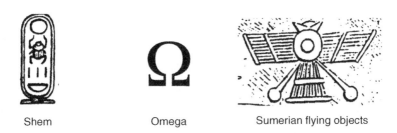

Shem   Omega   Sumerian flying objects

The Egyptian cartouche drawn here, indicates an omega in which a metamorphosis (scarab) is being carried out, thanks to the ascension of the module fastened to the ground by two moorings, like the Sumerian flying objects.[5] When an immortal arrives on Earth, won't they change clothing as well as form? What we consider to be legends of the past could become sad realities of tomorrow. At the end of a cycle, creatures flee dangerous places. Others, unconscious or fool-hardy, allow themselves to be shut up inside. This was us. Nevertheless, knowledge of the law of time allows us to understand that the future will drag us towards chaos only if we construct it ourselves and if we accept it in each one of our thoughts.

It is not a mistake to live where we can make use of survival instincts that we understand. Without a doubt, we need a little more time to get better at it and only the future offers us this possibility for long reflection. Nevertheless, it is important to understand the

---

4. Book of Genesis, VI 1-4.
5. See annex of Change your Future through the Time Openings.

workings of time, for when the moment comes near for us to finally come out of our burrow.

The Earth can be considered a paradise by those who ignore the law of times. For immortal creatures it is a hellish place where we live in the skin of a mortal animal, little by little becoming forgetful of the link with our double.

He is a being of light endowed with the creative strength of a star, which is our pole of re-unification and re-establishment. With him, how could we lack healthy information?

At the end of our doubling time, we will need instructions on how to survive, as the future, which we have created, will come to disturb us. At this very time, an envoy from the Creator is exploring the future to classify it and guide us. He knows the law of the alpha and the omega or the Oura, he is the envoy (el, elohim, elos) of this law, that is Oura-el.[6]

With his broom wagon he picks up the stragglers in the darkness, Ouriel is, according to tradition, the angel who proceeds from the infernal Tartarus. Doubled from the Creator, he recovers lost energy from the farthest time openings in the moment in which the Apocalypse opens our seven locks of time. Not understanding that an angel of God could come out of the darkness, the Christian church, plainly and simply, suppressed it from the Old Testament. Nevertheless, this envoy of the Creator is at the limit of the forbidden before disintegration. His passing disperses those who cannot come to their encounter with their double. We must therefore be preparing ourselves, if we don't want to become lost energy without consciousness of our unity.

---

6. Ουρα in Greek means the division of time (Ωρα), which separates the alpha α from the omega Ω, the furure from the past, uniting them through the link ρ. See Annex.

34
Who, When, How, Why?

It is almost midnight. An infinite tranquillity reigns in the country house where Aurelian's parents have invited us. Relaxed in our chaise-lounges, Charles and I silently contemplate the cloudless sky.

"Millions of stars," Charles exclaims dreamily, "and I, lost on one of them with my son who, after all, makes me understand my smallness."

"His story mustn't make you forget the essential. We have doubled in order to explore a dangerous solar space, lost in a galaxy in the middle of a limitless multitude of stars. A hundred thousand million stars in our galaxy and a hundred thousand million galaxies in our universe...If we had to count the stars, using a thousand millionth of a second for each one of them, do you know how long it would take us?"

"I suppose it would be unimaginable!"

"Three million years! That is, without a doubt, the reason why the Creator differentiates time, in order to take the time to know his creation. His visitations to a space like ours are not very frequent, at the most every 25,000 years. And besides that, He has to feel interested! Each time, our star opens and again closes its twelve planetary doors, every 180 years, separating for 24,840 years the troublemakers whom we are from the immortal creatures. Like Cinderella, we have to leave before the clock strikes twelve..."

"So, a lot of us get caught in our own trap."

"Only the Neanderthals seem to have escaped from our solar prison at the end of the last cycle. Since then, we have been cut off from the Creator, whose existence and oneness are, nevertheless, a scientific obligation of time and space. Although this displeases savage intellectuals..."

"Like me!" Charles interrupts smiling. "Anyway, I have ended up accepting all your sayings..."

"Which other people accept from the beginning, at times intuitively...just so you know that this famous *cutting off* isolates us from healthy information from the Creator and that contrary to well-established premises, God knows nothing about us, He sees nothing at all and hears almost nothing during the entire time of doubling."

"Now that's difficult to accept!"

"In 25,000 years, He receives information about our destiny, through the twelve immortal incarnations: the famous *avatars*. The Greek meaning, that I have given you of this important word, has been lost long ago. These necessary periodic visitations give us a certain vitality back, but unfortunately do not hinder humanity from constructing dangerous future possibilities that we must annul time and again...Updateable in every moment, those future potentials make up an enormous *load* that can impede our re-unification at the end of the *doubling time*. Nevertheless, we can always wipe away what we have created. It is enough to have our double with us along with his power of synthesis."

"Seeing that we have come here altogether, to become flesh and blood upon this earth in the last moment, wouldn't it be because we think we are capable of shaking off this weight?"

"Of course, but we no longer even know the how or the why. And on top of that, we aren't even aware of the need we have of a guide like Yeshua, whose historic and planetary importance you have already seen. How can we not consider the curiosity of the immortals when a space like ours is finally opened in their time? Perceiving the imperceptible allows each creature to see all possibilities: past, present and those yet to come!"

"It's true," adds Charles, "that if we were able to make the precise date of that final opening known, that would allow us to more quickly direct our lives. We would finally leave the trap that creates the current planetary misinformation for us."

"I have already told you that it is impossible to know the exact date of the end of times. It is certainly near and our incarnation on Earth at this crucial epoch is not a coincidence. Its sole purpose is to allow our double to arrange the future that we have *bothered* since the dawn of time. We are a springboard for him. By letting him sweep out our future potentials each day, we can repel the dangers and in this case, the end would bring about benefits."

"Arrange, without bothering, the future seems difficult."

"It is, nevertheless, the only way to eliminate the current foreseeable chaos. The Apocalypse would then once again find its etymological sense as *the marvellous discovery of the unknown*. The rising levels of the oceans, global warming, climatic changes, and so many cataclysms that we wrongly consider to be natural, would little by little disappear.[1] The Earth would only update the futures acceptable for everyone."

Charles adds "but who knows that? We are completely ignorant of our past."

"And so we create future potentials without any relation to this other *I* who should be our time messenger, that *anaguelos* well known to our Greek ancestors and not that cherub destroyed by

---

1. See annex of Change your Future through the Time Openings.

misunderstood esotericism. Not listening to him; we destroy him, and thereby breaking the image that the Creator wanted of us in the future. It will be very difficult to re-find our unity."

"Will the end of doubling time be the end of us?"

"We will be able to be one with our double provided that we do not run from him and we recognise him. If not, the light of his slowed-down time will push us towards the darkness of the future, where our terrestrial life has created an accelerated reality corresponding to our deepest desires, but totally useless to our double and therefore for ourselves. Remember the Gospel of Saint Thomas that I have spoken to you about. Its interpretation, without the more or less looked for contradictions of the medieval scribes, is *in the rough*: *When you make the two one, and when you make the inside like the outside and the outside like the inside, and the above like the below, and when you make the male and the female one and the same...then will you enter the kingdom.*"

"Do you mean to say that it is difficult to re-make our unity?"

"Everything depends upon the place where we re-make this unity! If we throw ourselves into a future, which doesn't correspond to the desires of our double, but to our own, he will be obliged to follow us when a new cycle of doubling begins. We will shut him up with us for 25,000 years, far from the Creator, in a space where he will become lost energy, a fallen angel, a mortal creature like those that currently parasitize our world leading us to chaos."

"Isn't a double always immortal?"

"No! If, at the end of doubling, we are lost in the future, he will be obliged to follow us, which is true death in the sense that he leaves the space of the Creator where he no longer has the vital synthesis. *If a man keep my saying,* said Jesus, *he shall never taste of death.*[2]

---

2. The Gospel According to Saint John, VIII 52.

This saying is understood if we know that a double in the past assures our relationship with the double of Yeshua, the known Paraclete, who, you will remember, finds his explanation in Greek and the doubling theory there. If our double remains in the past, he assures our survival in the space of the Creator, where there are numerous possibilities for exploration. That is how Yeshua protects us, trying to keep him alive in his space and time. The day before his death He again soothed us: *In my father's house are many mansions...I go to prepare a place for you.*[3] Our re-unification can take us to other spaces during the 1,080 years of transition between doubling cycles. It is a physical law and not an esoteric utopia."

"Do you think that Yeshua is a necessary guide during this new exploration of space?"

"Without him, it is impossible to find our body's survival instincts and the intuitions vital to our spirit. He allows us to abandon the useless in order to put the absolutely necessary into our explorer's rucksack: *and (those) which had not worshipped the beast, neither his image (in the future)... they lived and reigned with Christ a thousand years... This is the first resurrection.*[4] **Do you understand now that there is no legend nor dogma, not even the most minimal esoteric secret, only a rigorous scientific truth, which is, overall, accessible to everyone.** We have created the disorder. Let's let our doubles put things back into order, even if only to be able to survive the coming years!"

"Why wouldn't our death take us towards our double?"

"We must know the law of *going to sleep* and apply it successfully, exactly like Aurelian has known how to. Death is our last dream: first it takes us towards all the chimeras of the future that we have so much desired during our lives. It is necessary to know how to

---

3. The Gospel According to Saint John, XIV 2.
4. Book of Revelation, XX 4-5.

renounce them in order to be able to re-unite with the other part of ourselves. While waiting for this last moment, we are still on Earth, masters of the time openings and of those that create our future in the darkness. Extraterrestrials, hellish creatures are only denominations for the moment..."

"Denominations of poorly controlled origins..."

"Perhaps! This makes us under-estimate their importance and the real danger that they represent."

The object of our lives should be to attract to Earth future potentials compatible with the past of our double, however this in not the case.

It is more important to find the questions that were ours before having been born, than to resolve problems that have no interest for our double. That is why we must make use of the night to wipe away all that can be erased.

Finding balance consists in making the furthest future compatible with the furthest past, said our ancestors, the middle mu (mesos or messiah) between the alpha and the omega of our doubling. Yeshua tried this feat at the beginning of our era. He announced his return to us and to prove that he knew the law of time, like the Sumerian goddess Innana and the Egyptian god Horace, he resuscitated a body after three days for forty days. For him to come, without having to become incarnate, but in the united and glorious body at the end of time, one of our doubles will be obliged to be in relation to his.

Charles seems suspicious. "Can man be capable of renouncing what he thinks to be rational? For most people, this story of the double is difficult to accept, isn't it? Faced with strange things, modern man prefers to believe in the paranormal instead of imaging a possible scientific explanation, like yours..."

"And like our ancestors, who knowing the law of time, could see the future before having to live it. Isn't that the only way to expulse the tempting demons? Wouldn't the best therapist be the one who, like in the past, could state that he was a *Doctor of the Law, an exorcist and prophet*?"

"I can just imagine the reaction..." Charles bursts into laughter.

"Thinking wrongly, humanity ties itself to a dangerous future, abandoning a past that provides security. It is important to turn back before the sixth solar explosion, that sixth seal that is not at all mysterious, makes our time openings uncontrollable. As the doors to the past open last, we could suffer problems that we have created in the future before having our double's solution. He is the only one who can open the Creator's door for us."

It is delusional to look for planetary balance without taking the trouble to find personal balance.

35

The Final Trial

The extortionists were freed with only a protection order for Aurelian's school. He felt hemmed in and no longer wanted to go to school alone, but agreed to go with me.

"Carefreeness is a virtue," I tell this young man on the way to school. "One day I went to visit a countryman who lived on a farm that was quite far from the road. When I opened the gate, an enormous dog came up to lick my hand affectionately. I stroked him and slowly went down the muddy pathway. When I arrived to the farmhouse, I opened the door and went into the kitchen, accompanied by the dog. The family members, who were at the table eating, looked at me astonished. There was a dead silence. Do you know why?"

"Because you had entered without ringing?"

"No, because I had got to the house without any problem. The dog was very bad and everyone was afraid of him. No one had ever done what I had just done. The ferocious animal had probably not felt any aggression in me. What's more, I must admit, I was unaware of this danger."

"What does this have to do with me?" asks Aurelian. "My tormentors are worse than dogs!"

"The person who is afraid of a person or an animal will update to his everyday life a future capable of justifying that fear. He will become a potential adversary that the person or animal will try to push violently away, however it might be. Faced with a threat, fear grows and so attracts even more dangerous futures. If we understand this system, we can invert the cause and effect, deciding to no longer be afraid. Besides that, it is much more relaxing to update the desire to love an animal or a person who only our fearful thoughts have turned distrustful and aggressive."

"That's not possible, that's mad! I don't see myself loving those pigs!" objects the child.

"Man is no different from an animal: fear of a potential enemy engenders distrustfulness and reinforces enmity."

"What is enmity?"

"Let me explain: loving those who hate us can make one of them amiable. In reality, it's a question of always controlling our thoughts in order to create the best potential. It is not about love in the usual sense of the word. This control creates a potential energy, which is reinforced in the future and which everyone can make use of. This energy drives away the person who does not want it and who, therefore, continues to be your enemy. Nevertheless, showing a hypocritical friendliness or affection while hiding our true fear can only bring about aggressiveness from them, as the future only acts upon our real thoughts. It is true that frankness is not enough. To update the best potential, it is necessary to create it beforehand in order to be able to gather its fruits at the opportune time. As protection, you must have your affection and, overall, your honesty in the face of this affection, which mustn't be feigned. Appearances are useless, it is the being that matters, it is *to be*!

Aurelian makes an effort to smile. "The problem is that there are several possible updates and I don't have any."

"Only your momentary thoughts make you choose the correct one. It is up to you to watch over them and make the relationship between the acts that go with them. He, who never sees danger in the house of another, benefits from a great protection."

The child protests "I never saw it, before those blokes fell upon me! And anyway, there's no law for it."

"Of course there is! In the physics of the infinitely small, the observer is called a participant because he updates possibilities, which without his participation in the observation, would have no reality in his present."

"I'd rather be the participant in nothing at all, you know!"

"You are always the creator of that which you imagine about others. It is better to look for what pleases you instead of imagining a hostile environment. Think backwards and you'll live backwards. You always organise the disorders that you fear."

"But in this case, I haven't organised anything. I've suffered! Don't you realise what I've suffered?"

"When you think that the sun will wither the flowers in your garden, you start to make it shine. If you imagine a saving rain, clouds can come to your aid providing that a similar condition already exists in your future. What happens is that you normally keep time to an orchestra that does what it wants, imposing its music upon you. Your cells, a stone, the wind, the rain, a stream, a river, the ocean, flora, fauna are expecting the best futures from you. Your surroundings are too. Due to your thoughts and their updating, you are responsible for everything that surrounds you, the good as well as the bad."

Suddenly Aurelian gives an about face and walks quickly away. Surprised, I go after him.

"Can you tell me what this brusque turn around means?"

"There they are, at the corner, and I don't fancy updating or imagining anything. I'm going home. My cells, the wind, the rain, the entire Earth will wait until I calm down."

In the distance, the three troublemakers turn their backs towards us.

"Are you going to spend your whole life shut up in your burrow? You must face the dangers. Trust me! Get a move on! Prove to yourself that your thoughts are superior to your acts!"

Imploring me with his child's eyes, he stops in his tracks. "But then, what must I do?"

"Keep on going, while at the same time asking your double for protection. This protection only depends upon you thoughts."

To my great surprise, Aurelian heads back towards school, straight towards his tormentors who still haven't seen him. As I wish him to be totally responsible and think that he could turn around and ask me for help with a sad look, I leave in the opposite direction without turning around in order to show my absolute confidence in the future and in Aurelian's potential. A little further on I come upon Charles who was following us, nervous and ready to intervene. It is then that we both see Aurelian, standing as tall as justice, pass right by his tormentors who run away without causing trouble. Charles stands open-mouthed until the moment in which his son turns towards us with a broad smile and raises his arms in victory.

"That is almost unbelievable," says Charles stunned. "What have you said to him?"

"That if your double is with you, you run no risk."

"And if it hadn't helped him?"

"Why always think the worst, if it only makes it come true?"

Conclusion

"Have you prepared your conclusion well?" asks Aurelian, "because my teacher says that without a good conclusion, there is not a good text. And you know that many people read the end of the book first in order to find out if it's going to be interesting. And your book is much more than thrilling, it's revolutionary! Before reading it, I didn't know how I could create a good future for myself. It's brilliant!"

"The most brilliant is to know and repeat continually to whoever wants to listen to it that we update in every moment an existing future in order to live, knowing at the same time that this future can be very dangerous, given that it has been being created by everyone since 25,000 years ago. Nevertheless, I also know that the person who is able to maintain a relationship with their double, no longer suffers anguish, stress or doubt. If we become conscious of the danger, we will never again feed the fear that drags our world towards chaos. You should know that nobody impedes anyone from creating pleasant futures! But, of course, what is pleasant for me can be unpleasant for you. This I grant you."

"Except when you speak of the scientific thing, which shouldn't be forgotten," comments Aurelian who adds, sure of himself "*Do not think of doing to others what you don't want them to think of doing to you!* If not, be careful of damages in the future!"

"Do not forget to say that our double is always there and that he is the only one who can arrange the future that we have *upset*, providing that we let him help us!"

"No, don't say anything else, because at the end of the book the reader must still feel like more, otherwise she won't try to understand what I have understood. It's too much! She must discover it for herself."

"And what is this *too much* for you?"

"Being happy in every moment and knowing that my happiness brings about the happiness of my mother, my father, Octavia, my dog, my neighbour, my cells, the sea, the wind, the clouds...and even the galaxies...it is too brilliant! Overall if everyone is finally able to understand it...thanks to you and Lucile...and perhaps also thanks to a small young man like me!"

"Then control your thoughts in order to create the best potential knowing that you will never reach the limit."

Post scriptum

Neither moralising, nor criticising, this book's main objective is to provide you the help necessary in order to solve your problems without making anyone else, other than yourself, responsible.

Throughout this book we have tried to explain and make you understand the principal of the alpha and the omega, of the past and the future. A vital principal that assuredly leads us to controlling each one of our thoughts. It corresponds to you to say if this work has attained its principal objective, which means being useful and healthy along the road of your life.

Lucile and Jean-Pierre Garnier Malet

Made in the USA
Monee, IL
15 November 2024

70223327R00111